Praise for *Moe & Me*

For as great a golfer and legendary a personality as Moe Norman was, very few writers came to know the eccentric ball striker well. One person to truly call him a friend was Lorne Rubenstein and through a series of personal and poignant experiences in *Moe & Me: Encounters with Moe Norman, Golf's Mysterious Genius*, he finally shines the light on one of the game's best and most misunderstood figures.

— Bob Weeks, editor, *SCOREGolf*

For the last three decades, the only swings that PGA Tour players talked about with respect were Ben Hogan's and Moe Norman's. Lorne Rubenstein's sad and joyous book now guarantees that the pros will be talking about Moe for another thirty years.

— Bradley S. Klein, architecture editor, *Golfweek*, and author of *Discovering Donald Ross*

The strangest and most intriguing athlete I ever dealt with was golfing great Moe Norman. No one knew him better, or understood him more, than Lorne Rubenstein. *Moe & Me* is a compelling story that is part psychoanalysis, part tragedy, part comedy, part journey — and in all parts love. This is a unique and beautifully told story of a man who played the game like no golfer before or since. No one who ever met Moe ever forgot him. Those who meet him now through his friend Lorne will finally get to know the sporting world's most unforgettable character.

— Roy MacGregor, *Globe and Mail* columnist and author of *Wayne Gretzky's Ghost*

MOE & ME

MOE & ME

Encounters with Moe Norman, Golf's Mysterious Genius

LORNE RUBENSTEIN

ECW Press

Published by ECW Press
2120 Queen Street East, Suite 200, Toronto, Ontario, Canada M4E 1E2
416-694-3348 / info@ecwpress.com

Library and Archives Canada Cataloguing in Publication

Rubenstein, Lorne
Moe and me : encounters with Moe Norman, golf's mysterious genius / Lorne Rubenstein.

1. Norman, Moe, 1929–2004. 2. Golfers—Canada—Biography.
I. Title.

GV964.N67R83 2012   796.352092   C2011-906969-5

ISBN: 978-1-77041-053-4
also issued as: 978-1-77090-205-3 (PDF); 978-1-77090-206-0 (ePub)

Editor for the press: Jennifer Hale
Cover and Text Design: Tania Craan
Cover photo: © Don Vickery Photography
Front cover Tiger Woods quote: *Golf Digest*, January 2005
Printing: Webcom   5   4   3

The publication of *Moe & Me* has been generously supported by the Canada Council for the Arts which last year invested $20.1 million in writing and publishing throughout Canada, and by the Ontario Arts Council, an agency of the Government of Ontario. We also acknowledge the financial support of the Government of Canada through the Canada Book Fund for our publishing activities, and the contribution of the Government of Ontario through the Ontario Book Publishing Tax Credit. The marketing of this book was made possible with the support of the Ontario Media Development Corporation.

 Canada Council for the Arts / Conseil des Arts du Canada   Canada    ONTARIO ARTS COUNCIL / CONSEIL DES ARTS DE L'ONTARIO

Printed and bound in Canada

 FSC
www.fsc.org FSC® C004071
MIX
Paper from
responsible sources

ANCIENT FOREST ™
FRIENDLY

For Dick Grimm.
He's made Canadian golf better for years,
and I'm better for his long friendship.

CONTENTS

What is real but compassion as we move from birth to death?

— Greg Brown, "Rexroth's Daughter"

I'm just a different type of golfer, the
fastest player in the world, one look and whack.
It doesn't look like I'm trying. — Moe, 1987

INTRODUCTION

THERE WAS A STRANGE FEELING in the air at the 2004 Canadian Open. Something was missing. I was caddying for Richard Zokol, but his golf bag wasn't the heaviest thing I was carrying around with me.

Moe Norman was gone.

He died of congestive heart failure the Saturday before the tournament started at the Glen Abbey Golf Club. His voice was weak when we last spoke a few days earlier, but he was still playing six or seven holes a few times a week with his long-time pal, and four-time Canadian Amateur champion, Nick Weslock. Moe would hit a couple of balls down the fairway — always in the middle — and then knock them onto the green. He would get into a golf cart and drive to the green, but he wouldn't putt out. He would be out of breath after a few steps. His life was winding down. He spoke with his friend, the golf pro Mike Martz, the Thursday before he died. "Everybody has to die some-time, and it's been nice knowing you, pal," he told Martz.

The Canadian flag flew at half-mast at courses in and around his hometown of Kitchener over the weekend that Moe died and at Glen Abbey during the Canadian Open. The electronic leaderboards said, simply, "In memory of Moe Norman, 1929–2004." It had been a custom on the Tuesday of the tournament for Moe to saunter onto the practice tee, always at the request of players. Somebody, maybe Nick Price or Fred Couples or Vijay Singh, would invite Moe to hit balls. He'd say that he didn't have his clubs and that he was wearing street shoes. Inevitably, Moe would take a club from a player's bag, look at it, pronounce it a "matchstick" rather than something he could use, something he could feel, that had weight. Then he would start to hit a few balls, and soon he'd be in his own world. Players would watch, but they might as well not have been there. Moe was now himself; a golf club provided security for him. He'd been a ball-hitting wizard since he was a teenager.

The range felt empty that Tuesday without Moe. He'd planned to attend a dinner that night that the Royal Canadian Golf Association was holding to celebrate the 100th anniversary of the Canadian Open. Instead, ar-rangements were being made for visitation Wednesday and Thursday afternoons in Kitchener. The funeral would be held on the Friday of the tournament.

At Glen Abbey, I was returning to caddying after a twenty-two-year absence. Zokol was playing his only tournament of the year, and he had gone along with my idea of carrying his bag. We'd been friends since I'd started writing about golf twenty-five years before.

Storms hit Glen Abbey hard on Thursday, the first round of the tournament. We got in only seven holes. I was at the course before dawn on Friday. Zokol warmed up in the early morning darkness under klieg lights set up over the range. He finished his first round, shooting 75, and then played his second round. He shot 75 again and missed the cut. We talked a lot about Moe that long Friday, the day Moe was buried.

I felt uneasy. I'd wanted to attend Moe's funeral, but I had a job to do. It was one of those times when I wished I could have been in two places at once. Carrying Zokol's clubs, I thought of all the times I'd played with Moe and introduced him at clinics. I thought of the hours I'd spent in his company, driving around southern Ontario while he listened to motivational tapes. I remembered introducing him at a clinic on 9/11 at a tournament that raised money in support of programs to help those afflicted with autism; many people thought Moe was autistic. I wasn't sure about that, but he certainly was different. At that tournament, Moe sat in the clubhouse with the participants as the planes hit the twin towers. He managed that night to address the gathering from the vantage point of somebody who had made a life for himself in a game that didn't always accept him because of his differences. I too spoke. What could we say on such a day? Only that we must find a way to live together, whatever our differences.

I saw us driving around Calgary in his Cadillac — Moe bought a new Cadillac every year he could afford it. I remembered Moe stopping at clubs in Calgary where he felt welcomed and where he'd won the Canadian Amateur and Canadian PGA Championships. I remembered caddying for the Canadian golfer Jim Nelford at the 1981 Canadian PGA Championship at the Westmount Golf and Country Club in Kitchener, when Moe was in our threesome. Moe caddied there as a teenager until he tossed a member's clubs into a tree when he was insulted by the small tip. Westmount booted him from his job but had long since made peace with him and hosted a reception after the funeral. Sixty years had passed.

I remembered meeting Moe when I was a teenager myself. We connected over the mystery of the golf swing, except that he had seemed to solve the mystery with his idiosyncratic swing that was already famous — and baffling to most anybody who tried to study and emulate it. I remembered the late Canadian golfer George Knudson, a master of ball control himself, telling me that Moe was the most sensitive golfer I would meet and that I should be careful writing about him. George also said, of Moe's swing, "It's good today, it's good 100 years from now, it's not an issue. That's what's called quality."

I went home after lugging Zokol's bag for twenty-nine holes that Friday, and I was exhausted. But I wanted to spend a couple of hours reading the emails I'd received since Moe had died. There were many.

Moe was gone. I felt bereft. I read the letters. And reread them. A woman whose late father was close to Moe remembered when Moe had called her father from the Masters. She could still hear the voice of her father as he spoke with Moe. "No, Moe, you can't sleep in a sand trap at the Masters; you have to get a motel room." A fellow who used to play frequently with Knudson remembered when George told him, "In 1955 and 1956, Moe was the best golfer in the world, period." A New Yorker wrote, simply, "So sorry to hear of his passing. Remarkable man." A member of the Brantford club where Moe had played a couple of times a week recalled that his wife knew nothing about golf, but she knew of Moe; the couple was at the club one day when the gentleman spotted Moe's car in the parking lot, and he called his wife over to look inside because he knew it would be full of clothes and equipment. His wife couldn't get over this and called her husband "Old Moe" from that day on whenever she saw some clothes in his car. One fellow informed me that Moe had given him a tee that he had used to hit twenty-nine consecutive drives without the tee falling to the ground. An old friend of mine told me that he'd had putting problems years ago and had asked Moe for a tip. Moe told him to keep pushing the butt of his left hand down the line he chose and then took him to his car. He opened the trunk of his Cadillac and said, "Take any putter you like. I have to help my friends. You have to help your friends."

Moe touched golfers everywhere, and he reached them. He reached me. He still does. What was it about Moe? What *is* it about Moe?

Fairways look like deserts to me, even if
they're only thirty yards wide. Look at this ball.
It'll fit, won't it? — Moe, 1989

MEETING MOE

IN THE EARLY 1960S, when Arnold Palmer was dominating golf and Arnie's Army was following him, I was thirteen years old and encountered Moe Norman for the first time. He was working at the De Haviland Golf Centre in north Toronto, a five-minute drive from where I lived. Moe's responsibilities included teaching and selling equipment and, generally, just hanging around De Haviland, which featured a two-tier driving range, a huge practice green, a nine-hole course, a thirty-six-hole mini-putt course, and a night-lit, par-three, eighteen-hole course. After some difficulties on the PGA Tour, which I'll discuss in the next chapter, Moe had found some peace here. He was comfortable among people who came to De Haviland for practice and play. I first remember Moe behind the counter dispensing white wire pails of yellow golf balls to golfers. Small pails. Medium. Large. Beaten-up drivers whose heads were scratched filled the racks behind Moe. He grabbed the pails of balls from the bins behind him. In between customers, this red-faced man in his tangerine shirt, banana slacks and torn golf shoes through which his toes stuck out flashed his snaggled teeth, sharp as the tines of forks, and performed card tricks. I watched. Moe was friendly. He told me to hit some balls.

"Go on, go on, it's a nice night, it's a nice night," he said. "It's warm. It's warm. Maybe I'll hit some too."

I walked out the door to the night and put a pail down by the hitting station. Moe emerged a few minutes later, holding his driver and bouncing a ball off the clubface. He walked slowly to a station with a pail of balls. He then placed a ball on the rubber tee embedded in the hitting area. The rubber tee popped up as if it jumped from underground. His head snapped left as he looked quickly down the vast, grassy area flecked with balls. The sky was black, but the klieg lights turned night into day. Moe set his clubhead a foot behind the ball. I wondered why. He looked unlike any other golfer I'd seen. Who sets the club a foot behind the ball? Only Moe, I would learn. He spread his feet well apart — although not as far apart as he would later in his life — so that it appeared he was trying to do the splits. Moe extended his arms out so far in front of him, with his hands held so unusually high, that I thought they could pop out of his shoulders. He looked like a lion awakening from slumber.

Moe did more than hit balls off the rubber tees. His real show started when he hit balls off the asphalt that extended the entire width of the range, 100 yards or more. Moe picked the ball cleanly off the asphalt with a driver. His contact with the ball was so clean that he didn't leave a nick on the driver's soleplate. How was that possible?

Moe moved the club back low and slow and returned it through the ball low and long. His arms and the club were a unit, like one of those triangles used to set balls on a snooker table. The clubhead pointed down the range as if it were tracking the flight of the ball. His ball flew straight, an arrow. Then, hardly stopping, he hit another ball. Same routine, same result. Balls continued to fill the night sky like sparklers. They were tracers, and I was mesmerized. Other golfers had stopped hitting balls and walked over to watch Moe. He was sweating, hitting one ball after another. He talked while he hit.

"Hope and fear, hope and fear, that's how people play golf," Moe said and thwacked another ball dead straight. "Not me. No, not me. I see happiness, I see happiness." He was drenched in sweat, and he was speaking as quickly as he was swinging, words flying out of his mouth like popcorn out of a popper. "The ball fits the Moe Norman way."

I lived a mile away, and I went to De Haviland with my father a few nights a week. We hit balls, and we played the par-three course with my dad's pals, including a fellow named Sam Shapiro. Sam showed up at De Haviland one day because he wanted to learn how to play golf. He ran into Moe and asked where he could take some lessons.

"You've come to the right place," Moe told Sam, who took more than fifty lessons from him.

"I had a good relationship with Moe," Sam said. "I liked him. He was a nice guy, and he would give you his heart. I went to Florida with him, and we'd go into restaurants to eat, but he wouldn't stay inside. He would take a sandwich, put it in his pocket, and eat outside. You had to feel for him. I'm not a doctor, but he was a human being." Moe taught Sam so well that he got down to a single-digit handicap, and he had a short game that turned bogies into pars regularly. Sam stayed close to Moe and attended his funeral.

As much golf as my dad and I played at De Haviland, we spent more time watching Moe. He fascinated me not only because of his extraordinary ability to control the flight of the ball, the true art of the game, but also because he was so different from every other golfer I'd seen. Moe looked like no other golfer I'd come across, nor did his style resemble that of any other golfer. He never took a practice swing — he never took a practice swing his entire life — but every shot flew dead straight, virtually without any sidespin. Even the best players in the world hit the ball with some sidespin. Moe hit the ball so that it rotated as if it were a Ferris wheel. He could also curve the ball at will. He could hit the ball high or low and everything in between. Moe knew where the ball was going. When somebody asked him to hit it to a specific spot, he hit it there.

"I make narrow holes look wide," Moe told me. "I never get tired of the middle. It's beautiful there." The faces of his irons were worn with a spot the size of a quarter in the center, equidistant from either side. He liked to show people the spots. Moe craved adulation. He needed approval.

Moe was in his early thirties when I first encountered him, drifting that summer from course to course and tournament to tournament, as he would the rest of his life. It was immediately apparent that he was like nobody else I'd met. By being himself, Moe stood alone.

I don't know why Moe galvanized my attention to the degree he did. I was a shy kid myself and didn't socialize easily. Maybe the few incidents that I remember from when I was a youngster are the ones that made me sympathetic to Moe when I met him.

Before I met Moe, I attended a Hebrew day school in Toronto. We studied Hebrew and Jewish history for half a day, and the conventional public school education in Ontario filled the other half. I enjoyed the intense focus on academic subjects but also missed sports, for which there wasn't a lot of time. I followed sports closely, though, and was paying more attention to the seventh game of the 1960 World Series than perhaps I should have been. The Pittsburgh Pirates were at home playing the New York Yankees at Forbes Field. I brought a transistor radio to class and carefully tucked it into my pocket. I listened to the game through an ear bud in my left ear and leaned forward to listen to the teacher. My left hand covered my ear. The score was 9-9 as the Pirates took to the plate in the bottom of the ninth inning. Their second baseman, Bill Mazeroski, was leading off. He hit a walk-off home run that has been called the most famous home run in baseball history. Nobody had ever hit a walk-off home run to win a World Series. I rose up from my desk as soon as the ball left the park. The teacher wasn't pleased and came over to rap me on my neck with the back of his hand. The pleasure I felt while listening to the game was worth the punishment.

A few weeks later I decided that I wanted more sports in my life and left the school for a nearby public junior high. The school had a proper baseball diamond and an ice rink. I played for the football team, called the Red Devils. Meanwhile, in my first gym class, I noticed a boy whose first name was the same as mine. He was standing in a corner away from the other students. He didn't want to participate in any of the activities. Clearly, he was different. He was gay, although nobody used that word then. Classmates called him a "fairy" and a "homo." They laughed at him. He felt even more apart, even lonelier. I tried to be kind to him, maybe because we shared a first name or maybe because I thought my classmates shouldn't be ridiculing him. He was different, true. But so what? Let him be.

I'd reached my adult height of six foot three by the time this happened, and I was always the tallest kid in class. I felt apart from other students and didn't mix easily. At school parties, I faded to the margins. At dances, I stood by the wall — the classic "wallflower." I took refuge in sports, especially golf. Although I was a fair athlete in hockey, baseball, football and soccer, golf provided me with a place where I could most be myself. I felt a freedom on the course that I felt nowhere else. A golf course provided a refuge. Golf was a way into myself and, therefore, a way out of myself. Was it that way for Moe, only much more so? I was too young to be able to formulate such questions consciously, let alone answer them. But something in Moe captured my attention.

Night after night I went to De Haviland, usually with my father. He'd played pro football in Winnipeg, his hometown, but had given it up after a knee injury. Now he had a small automotive supplies store. He loved sports, and he saw that I had some talent for golf. I played the Ontario Junior and won a provincial team event with the pro at the club where I played. Other kids were going out with friends or to summer camp or the local Dairy Queen for ice cream. We called it the Puppy Palace. I spent many more evenings at De Haviland than at the Puppy Palace because of Moe. I didn't know it then, but I would chase the truth of the man from then on. I would chase it through university as I acquired a master's degree in psychology, and I would chase it while I caddied on the PGA Tour a few tournaments each summer while I was in university, and I would chase it after I became a golf writer. I would chase it until Moe died, and I'm still chasing it.

Always there was Moe, flitting along the fringes of the game, owning his swing or, as he said, "capturing" it. Always I would find him, and follow him, and meet him, and write about him. I watched him at De Haviland. I followed him in tournaments. Later, after I started writing, I argued, along with other colleagues, that Moe should be an inductee into the Canadian Golf Hall of Fame, and when he was finally admitted in 1995 I was at the ceremony at Foxwood, a small rural club where Moe felt comfortable.

I told Moe Norman stories everywhere I traveled in golf; his name always came up. Everybody knew Moe or of him. Everybody was curious about him.

Maybe it was because I felt some kind of kinship with Moe, but I never ridiculed him in private or public. Some writers called him the Clown Prince of Canadian Golf or Sleepy Moe from Hollow Norman — a description that appeared when he was playing out of the Sleepy Hollow Club near Toronto. An English writer called him a "nutter of imperial status." He even called himself Moe the Schmo.

Moe hit the ball cleanly and accurately with a swing that appeared to defy convention. Yet he never succeeded on the game's biggest stages. He was far too insecure for that; professional golf is a private game played publicly, and Moe couldn't cope with its public side until late in his life — and even then not easily or comfortably. After he won the 1955 Canadian Amateur in Calgary, he hid by the bulrushes on the banks of the Bow River rather than give a speech at the prize ceremony. He could address a crowd many years later, but mostly he spoke by rote, reciting material he'd memorized — usually the same material. Life was never easy for Moe. But he cruised along, finding his way.

On the course, Moe had control of the golf ball if nothing else. The course was the one place where he was able to exert mastery. He loved being on a course or on a range or in his car, listening to tapes about the psychology of golf.

Moe was ill at ease in social situations and tried to avoid them. The practice range, the golf course, his car, and his motel room were his natural, chosen places; he couldn't cope with the social side of the game. I was at a cocktail party at the Glen Abbey Golf Club in Oakville, Ontario, as part of Jack Nicklaus's induction into the Canadian Golf Hall of Fame in the builder category; Nicklaus had designed Glen Abbey, home of the Canadian Open from 1977 to 2000, with the exception of 1980 and 1997 when it was held at the Royal Montreal Golf Club. Moe was invited, and he stood wearing a red sports jacket. The bar was crowded, and he was trapped. Suddenly, I heard my wife, Nell, yelp; Moe, trying to be friendly, had come up behind her and put his glass of ice-cold Coke against the back of her neck as a way of saying hello. "Somebody told me you're Lorne's wife. Just want to say hello."

Another time Moe was sitting outside a clubhouse when a golfer came along. He was going in for lunch and asked Moe if he wanted anything. Moe said he'd like some ice cream. The member went inside and asked for some ice cream for Moe. He was told ice cream wasn't available and went outside to tell Moe. "Sorry, they have no ice cream." Moe said, "I know. You asked what I wanted, and I said ice cream." To Moe, this was the right answer. He wanted ice cream. He hadn't asked the club member to get him ice cream.

His reactions didn't depend on where he was or to whom he was talking. Craig Shankland, a PGA Master professional who was close to Moe for the last eighteen years of his life, went with him to the Bay Hill Club in Orlando to do a clinic for a medical company. Arnold Palmer owned Bay Hill and drove toward Moe and Shankland near the driving range, where they were to conduct their clinic.

Palmer said, "Hi, how are you, Moe?" Moe knew that Palmer, seven-time major champion that he was, wasn't the most accurate striker of a golf ball. Moe came right back to Palmer's friendly greeting with "I haven't had a thorn bush stuck up my ass for the last seven years, how about you, Arnie?" Palmer didn't know what to say for a moment, and then, Shankland remembered, he "began to crack up, ending on the floor of his cart, tears coming from his eyes, doubled up with laughter."

Moe reacted immediately to situations. He lacked a trip wire or filter. This wasn't helpful in social situations, but it was valuable in golf. Moe turned golf into a reaction sport rather than a creation sport. He played golf as if it were hockey or baseball; he was reacting rather than initiating a motion. Moe looked at the target, assimilated all the information he needed, and swung immediately: his swing was his reaction. All golfers want to play the game without thinking. His nature compelled him to play that way. That's why he hated blind shots, where he couldn't see the target.

Moe occupied a cubbyhole all his own, and he made that space his world. The sport at which he excelled forced him to encounter the world beyond the spaces he preferred to occupy. Yes, he lived in the golf world, but he never did truly occupy it. There was always something impermanent about his place there. The place where Moe could best express himself also imprisoned him. A driving range, a field in the countryside where he could hit balls, or his car at the side of a rural dirt road — these were his real homes, where he felt most at ease.

When I think about Moe, I think about a line from a Leonard Cohen song: "There's a crack in the world, that's how the light gets in." Moe represents a crack. By being in the world, he let some light in.

People laughed at me because I made it look so easy.

Sure they did. Sure they did. — Moe, 1993

BACKGROUND

MOE AND HIS TWIN SISTER, Marie, were born in July 1929 in Kitchener, Ontario, a blue-collar city of about 30,000 people an hour southwest of Toronto. He was one of three brothers and three sisters. Moe's father, Irwin, worked at Beaver Furniture in Kitchener as an upholsterer until automation ended that trade. He then became a shipper there. The family lived in a small home at the top of a hill on Gruhn Street, near Kitchener-Waterloo Collegiate. Stories were later written that the family was poor, but Marie denied that was the case. "I can't believe the things they've written in the paper," she said. "It was far from poverty. It sure upset my mother, the garbage they printed."

Moe and his friends loved to sleigh-ride down the hill

from the home at the top of the hill. He was five when he and his pal Jimmy Laflamme, riding double, tumbled down the hill on January 18, 1935, in the early afternoon. They went right under a car, which dragged them a short distance. Homer Berner, the driver, didn't see the boys as he approached. He managed to stop the car, but not before one of the rear wheels had come to rest on the sled. Moe and Jimmy appeared to be unhurt, although Moe did suffer a slight bruise to his cheek when he was thrown clear. The boys got up and ran home. Moe hid under the sofa in his house when a tall policeman came to investigate the accident.

It wasn't long before Moe started behaving differently at school. He started to speak very quickly, often repeating himself. It became apparent that one side of his face had been pushed up slightly. Marie said it had been "crushed. How much damage it did we don't know." Moe's mother, Mary, came to regret that she hadn't taken her son to the hospital for an examination.

In school, Moe found his subject, math, immediately. He was able to add long sequences of numbers and come up with the answers quickly. "That was the only subject I was smart at," he told me. "I could say seven sevens are forty-nine; forty-six and fifty-six are 102. The rest of the stuff, subjective completions, copula verbs, who discovered this, I wasn't good at." But Moe was able to spell, and, contrary to what people would later think, he was able to read. Moe didn't like to write, though, because he was left-handed and desks were made for right-handers. He smeared the page with ink, which bothered him. Moe was given a pencil to use, but he never did like the act of writing.

But he did like sports, and later, when he focused on golf, he carried notes about the game in his own neat, childlike handwriting. While in school, Moe played baseball and hockey. In baseball, he had an uncanny ability to hit the ball precisely where he wanted. Moe hit .610 one summer in organized baseball to lead the league. He hit mostly singles, picking holes in the infield and driving the ball between fielders. Although he enjoyed hockey and baseball, he found his sport in golf. Moe started to caddy when he was ten at the posh Westmount Golf and Country Club in Kitchener. Some of his friends were making sixty cents a round caddying there. He liked the possibility of making some money while being outdoors, and the game appealed to him. "You know how you are as a kid," he said. "You're walking on a beautiful piece of grass. I loved it."

Moe soon fashioned a club from the limb of a tree at a park near his home. The limb was curved at one end, so he could use it as a golf club. A member at Westmount for whom he had caddied gave him a five-iron two years later. Moe said it was like going from a Volkswagen to a Cadillac, and he started to whack balls around the park. By the time he was twelve, about the only things he did at his family home were eat and sleep. He was seventeen when he left home, and then he lived in a succession of motel rooms. He did come home from time to time. "My parents always said they could hear him in the attic, crawling around," Moe's youngest brother, Richard, told me. "They always thought he had money up there."

When Moe was a youngster, there were two houses on the other side of a park across from his house, about 150 yards away. He liked to get up early and start his day by hitting a couple of balls between the houses. The residents heard the golf balls clattering when they landed and complained. Moe broke eleven windows in two years while hitting golf balls; two were broken on the same day. His parents insisted that he stop hitting balls between the houses.

Meanwhile, Moe feared his father, who, he always maintained, didn't want him to caddy at Westmount or play golf. He said his father thought golf was a "big shot's game." Moe so feared his father that he dug a hole in front of the house and buried his clubs there. "They told me to play a man's game. Play hockey. Play football. I got no encouragement. None at all." Moe wiggled his way into the hole he'd dug to retrieve the clubs and kept his intense feelings about golf to himself. He also played hooky from school every Thursday morning, when the caddies were allowed to play Westmount. "I was tickled to be there," Moe told me. "On the first tee, I was shaking. I was afraid to hit the ground. It was so beautiful. I didn't want to damage the property." But his family didn't know how he felt about the game. "You never knew what Moe was thinking," Marie told me. "He would eat and leave. My mom and dad couldn't get real close to him."

His relationship with his father was strained. Moe said that he used one end of a golf club to hit the ball and that his father used the other end to hit him. He claimed that his father never saw him hit a golf ball, although Marie and

Richard say that wasn't true and that his feelings reflected his insecurity more than reality. His father once came to watch him play in the Kesselring Field Day at Rockway, a municipal course near the Norman home. This was a big tournament in its time, and 2,000 spectators turned up to watch the best amateurs of the day. Some top Americans played in it.

Soon after finding golf, Moe began to drift away from his family and into his own world. He snuck onto Westmount some afternoons, beginning when he was fourteen, and Moe was soon winning tournaments against other caddies. He skipped school regularly in the afternoons so that he could golf or caddy, and at night he set pins in The Strand, a local bowling alley. Moe resented being in school and tightened up around people. He felt at home only on the golf course. Caddying and playing golf became his life. When he was in school, he sometimes told his teachers that he would be rich one day. They didn't know what to make of him. They wondered what would become of him. His formal education ended at fourteen when Moe was expelled from school for missing classes. His mother always felt she could tell when he played hooky and was on the course, because there were grass stains on the bottom of his pant legs; he played frequently and hit balls when he wasn't on the course. Rockway's pro, Lloyd Tucker, noticed Moe — it was impossible not to notice him — and encouraged him to continue, for the most part, his method of swinging. Rockway was also where, a few years later, Moe met Gus Maue, who, along with his wife, Audrey, would come to play a prominent role in his life — so much so, in fact, that they would handle his banking, and Audrey would do his laundry. Maue was only twelve years old and helping Tucker at Rockway when he first saw Moe, who was seven years older. Moe, he said, liked him. A few years later Maue started picking up the range balls that Moe was hitting during practice. He went on to become a professional at various clubs, including Westmount.

A membership to Rockway cost twenty-five dollars. Moe handed over fifty cents whenever he could afford it from his earnings at Westmount until he paid for his membership. There was no television in his house until the 1950s, but Moe heard about golf beyond Rockway and Westmount from the *Kitchener-Waterloo Record*, the local paper. He learned about Ben Hogan and Sam Snead and Jimmy Demaret and the legendary amateur Bobby Jones. Jones had retired in 1930, when he was twenty-eight, after winning the then Grand Slam: the U.S. and British Opens and Amateurs. Moe said to himself, "Wouldn't I like to hit the ball like him someday?"

Moe wasn't the only excellent young golfer at Rockway. He thought that smooth-swinging Gerry Kesselring was better than he was. He was wary of Gary Cowan, who had started to caddy at Rockway when he was ten years old. Cowan's swing was short, fast and powerful. (Cowan eventually won the 1961 Canadian Amateur and the 1966 and 1971 U.S. Amateurs; Kesselring won the 1946 and 1947 Canadian Juniors, four Ontario Amateurs, and four Ontario Opens.) Tucker brought each youngster along by keeping the boys apart on the lesson tee; he respected their individual styles. The only thing that mattered was the flight of the ball, not how the swing looked. But Cowan knew more than that mattered when it came to success on the professional tour. He said Moe had an inferiority complex second to none. Moe had plenty of friends when he was a youngster, but, he claims, "They called me sissy, playing golf. What sort of a sport was golf? You hit a ball, and you walk after it. That's not a sport." Then there was the way Moe looked, wearing torn shoes, pants that were too big for him or too short. "I heard people say, 'Here comes the tramp.'" Later, when he was winning amateur tournaments, he heard more of the same. "Here comes the guy who sleeps in the shithouse, the guy who sleeps in bunkers. I heard all this stuff. I heard all this stuff. I kept it inside myself."

Moe stayed with golf and with his style. He stood out. But who knows what would have transpired had Tucker advised Moe to develop a more conventional swing? Who knows what would have happened had he not encouraged Moe to go his own way? Moe's favorite song was Frank Sinatra's "My Way." Had Moe gone anybody else's way, he might have lost his game entirely. It's impossible to imagine Moe standing conventionally to the ball and swinging in a more standard way. Yet his way, coupled with his personality, led him to become golf's loner. Golf gives loners freedom of expression. Moe expressed himself through golf. He expressed himself into a cocoon where it was difficult for anybody to reach him.

"Golf was an individual, not a team, thing," Moe said.

"It's just me. If I wanted to get out there, I'd get out there. That was very appealing to me. Nobody is allowed to touch your ball. Nobody can make you look good. In hockey, if a defenceman backchecks, he can make you look good. In golf, it's just you. It's just you, mister."

Moe hitchhiked from tournament to tournament and often slept in fields. One Sunday morning the family came downstairs and saw a television in the living room. Moe had won the television and simply placed it there and moved on. "He just put it there," his brother Richard said, smiling, "and carried on with his business. That was his way." Moe didn't wait around to see how his parents would react upon seeing the television. He had made his point by putting it in the living room and then leaving the house. His silence was eloquent.

Moe didn't own a car until he was twenty-six. He won that 1955 Canadian Amateur, which got him an invitation to the 1956 Masters. George Knudson said years later that nobody in golf was hitting the ball better than Moe in those days. "Pick the best players then, [Cary] Middlecoff, Palmer, Hogan. I would have taken his ball against their best from tee to green," he told me. "He was the greatest I'd seen. He had blade angle covered, he's got a solid base, and he's not afraid to move." Knudson was impressed with the factors that made Moe's swing work. The clubface would return to the ball square to the ball flight Moe wanted because he didn't twist it during his swing. He was rooted to the ground during his swing, and he was so solidly in place that he could swing away from the ball and back through. As Knudson noticed, Moe wasn't afraid to move while swinging.

Moe was living in a motel room in Kitchener and working at The Strand bowling alley when the invitation to the Masters arrived at his parents' home. "I was setting up pins one night when it's ten below outside," Moe said, "and when I got home here's this invitation to the Masters. What a thrill." Moe and Irv Lightstone, then an amateur and later the head professional at the Maple Downs Golf and Country Club north of Toronto, drove to the Augusta National Golf Club with Kenny Jacobs, another local pro. On the way down, they played some tournaments and stayed in a rooming house in Brunswick, Georgia. They met Paul Bumann, a young man who'd been the captain of the golf team at Notre Dame University. Bumann, then twenty-five, was the pro at the Brunswick Country Club and a trick-shot artist. He was called the Clown Prince of Golf because of his trick-shot artistry. His nickname was the same one some writers thought was appropriate for Moe, although for different reasons. Jim Barclay, in his scholarly book *Golf in Canada: A History*, referred to Moe as Canada's Clown Prince of Golf because of his on-course behavior. As Barclay pointed out, Moe did clown his way around a course. At least that was how those who played with him and watched him interpreted his actions. But he was just being Moe. He wasn't a trick-shot artist, even if he did hit 250-yard drives down the throat of the fairway off Coke bottles and four-inch tees. He was an artist.

Bumann invited Moe, Irv and Kenny to play at his

club. They took advantage of the opportunity. Off the course, they found a general store in the middle of town where they could order food and play pool. Their dinner every night was a chili dog, fries and a Coke. Meanwhile, they needed some money to continue their journey. "Moe told me to call information in Palm Beach and get the number for Conn Smythe. He'd send us some money," Irv said. Smythe owned the Toronto Maple Leafs and Maple Leaf Gardens, and he gave Moe some money. It wasn't the first time. Moe's brother Richard was at Westmount in Kitchener one day with Smythe, and he saw the hockey impresario shove his hand into Moe's pocket, to Richard's surprise. "I can still see him putting his hand in Moe's pocket," Richard told me. "That night I asked Moe why he did that, and Moe pulled out the money."

Moe and Irv arrived at Augusta National well before the other players. Kenny had some heart problems and wasn't feeling well, so he had returned to Toronto. Moe wanted to stay with Lightstone in a motel, but the club insisted that its amateur participants in the Masters stay in the Crow's Nest, a warren of tiny rooms in the clubhouse. Ken Venturi, who would go on to win the 1964 U.S. Open, remembers that Moe upset members when he hit full iron shots off the practice putting green. The members thought he was ripping up the green, but he picked the ball so cleanly off the turf that he didn't leave a mark. As he liked to say about the shape and depth of divots, "bacon strips, not pork chops, bacon strips, not pork chops."

Moe wanted to get right out and play his first day at

Augusta National. He grabbed his clubs and walked down the first fairway, carrying them, as he did at home. A couple of staff members came out and asked what he was doing. Moe told them he was carrying his bag, which he preferred to do. But, as he told me, he also didn't have enough money to pay a caddy for the four tournament days of the Masters. He was preserving his cash during practice so that he could pay a caddy during the tournament. "I didn't want to get into trouble because I couldn't pay my caddy," he said. "No way."

Moe was told he couldn't carry his own clubs, even in a practice round. Lightstone was walking with him, and they were over the hill on the first fairway and beyond the bunker on the right when they saw club and tournament co-founder Clifford Roberts approaching them in a cart. Moe knew who he was. Roberts said he would go with him so that he could be provided with a caddy. They returned to the clubhouse, although Moe told him he didn't have enough money for a caddy until the tournament. The club provided him with one anyway.

Moe was jittery when his turn came to drive off the first tee in the opening round. Spectators, or "patrons," as Augusta National calls them, surround the first tee no matter whether a player's name is Moe Norman or Greg Norman. It's a mark of respect for the golfers who have been invited to play the Masters. But hardly anybody knew anything about Moe.

"I was shaking like a leaf," Moe said. I can imagine him shuffling to the first tee from the practice putting green a few yards away, as if hoping nobody would notice him.

Suddenly, he was there, not a moment too soon for the starter to announce him. "Fore please, M—" thwack! "—urray Norman driving."

"Before they could say my name, bang, I hit it down the middle," Moe told me. He had not so much quelled his fear as he had refused to let it surface, and he'd done so by playing his way: put the ball on the tee, glance down the fairway, and zap, let it fly.

Moe shot 75 and 78 in the first two rounds. There was no cut then, so he went to the range to hit balls after his second round. He was hitting balls there when Sam Snead had a look at his swing. Snead had already won three Masters and had the silkiest swing in golf. He was struck by Moe's unusual style. He gave Moe some advice, and Moe betrayed his insecurity by taking it and then hitting some 800 balls to try to perfect Snead's suggestions. Years later, when I spoke with Moe about this, he remembered the story in a different way than it's been told. "Here you are, just a kid, getting a lesson from the man with the best tempo of anybody who ever played the game, with a beautiful swing. He gave me a lesson, and like a dummy I go out the next morning, hit 800 balls, and my thumb swells up so I couldn't put pressure on [it]."

It doesn't seem possible that Moe hit those 800 balls the morning before his third round, because, as he said, it took him four hours to hit that many balls. Nobody, even Moe, would hit that many balls before a tournament round; for one thing, he would have dominated the spot on the range for too much time. Did Moe, understandably after so many years, forget when he spent those four hours on Augusta National's range? Or did he tell the story as he did to embellish it? He wouldn't have had even the night before to try to heal. Was Moe helping to create his own legend? I've learned over the years that he didn't always remember significant events accurately or that he intentionally related them differently than they happened. And the 1956 Masters story has become such an integral part of Moe's legend, that the facts, as far as they can be known, have probably become apocryphal.

Whatever the sequence of events, what was the point in Moe hitting so many balls in the middle of the Masters? He'd hit hundreds of thousands of balls in his life, maybe millions. His swing was as much a part of him as his arms and legs. He could no more change it than he could start speaking Spanish spontaneously. The graft couldn't take and didn't. But who was Moe Norman to refuse Sam Snead's advice? That was exactly the point. He was Moe Norman, and he knew how to paint the sky with golf balls flying every which way at his command. He already "owned" his swing, the word Tiger Woods would use years later to pay Moe the ultimate compliment.

At the same time, there is another interpretation of the Moe and Snead story. Henry Ransom, a Texan who won five PGA Tour events between 1946 and 1955, believed Snead may have had ulterior motives in offering advice to Moe. Duke Butler, a long-time PGA Tour executive, played for Texas A&M University when Ransom coached the golf team. Ransom told Butler that it's possible that Snead was toying with Moe, hoping the insecure Moe would take the bait of the "lesson" he was offering.

Moe played the third round with a left hand that could hardly touch a blade of grass without giving him pain, let alone grip and control a golf club. Every time Moe put his hands around the grip of a club, it was as if he were touching a hot element on a stove. He eventually split a thumb during the first nine holes and had to stop playing. He left Vic Ghezzi, with whom he was playing, on his own. It's been said that Moe walked off Augusta National because he couldn't cope with the atmosphere and felt uneasy. But he wasn't required to make a speech there or to do anything but play golf. He had achieved a dream by making the Masters. And then he had spoiled it by carving up his hands. We will never know with certainty why he did so. Still, Moe didn't abandon Ghezzi. He just couldn't play anymore. "Moe was in too much pain to go on," Irv Lightstone said. "That's all there was to it." Ghezzi joined the twosome ahead.

Moe returned to Kitchener and played the amateur circuit. He won seventeen of twenty-one tournaments that summer, including his second Canadian Amateur. Two tournaments kicked him out because he was clowning around. Augusta National again invited Moe to the Masters, and he shot 77–74 to miss the cut that had been instituted by then. When he returned home, the Ontario Golf Association scolded him for playing too quickly in a tournament and told him to slow down by zigzagging his way down the fairway. "The only way we'll tolerate your fast play is if you jaywalk the fairways," an official told him. "We don't want you walking a straight line."

Meanwhile, before the 1957 Masters, Moe had qualified for a national team that was going to play the 1956 Americas Cup in late October, a three-cornered match against the United States and Mexico. Moe had represented Canada at the event two years before and had beaten Bill Campbell. Campbell had already twice won the prestigious North & South Amateur in Pinehurst, North Carolina, and went on to win the 1964 U.S. Amateur and to be elected in 1990 to the World Golf Hall of Fame.

Moe had already been fitted for a team jacket for the 1956 Americas Cup when things started to go awry. Royal Canadian Golf Association president and team captain Jim Anglin, a lawyer from Vancouver, got a call one day from Marion Doherty. The RCGA's secretary informed Anglin that Moe was showing off an official letter demanding that he pay back taxes on his golf earnings. Anglin told me that the taxman wanted to know what the RCGA would do about that.

As an amateur, Moe wasn't allowed to earn any money from playing golf. But he sometimes gave clinics and passed the hat for donations. The authorities had learned of this — hence the letter. Moe had violated his amateur status. Anglin was going to Toronto and advised Doherty that she should get the Ontario Golf Association's president and secretary to the RCGA's downtown office on Bay Street. Moe was playing in OGA events, and Anglin judged that it was that association's responsibility to investigate the matter. At the meeting, Anglin said, "He's your boy, it's up to you. What are you going to do about it?" He recalled that the OGA officials didn't say anything. "I told them it's their job, but I'll have to investigate it." In Anglin's view, the OGA was afraid to stick its neck out because Moe was a drawing card. He said the OGA should ensure that Doug Bajus, the first alternate, should be ready to leave with the team.

Moe was proud of the money he'd earned, and he wasn't shy about showing the letter around. A rumor that Conn Smythe was supporting Moe with financial aid had also gone around, although there wasn't any confirmation. The rumor was fact, as Irv Lightstone and Moe's brother Richard confirmed to me. This violated the amateur code by which golfers were supposed to pay their own expenses. Anglin tried to reach Moe to discuss the matter. Anglin left messages at his parents' home and sent telegrams to him. Moe didn't return the messages, so Anglin, along with the RCGA's Robbie Robinson, drove out to Kitchener and waited outside the house for Moe to appear. His mother said he had left for the bowling alley. Anglin and Robinson tried to find him there but were told Moe had gone to a local hockey rink. He wasn't there either. Anglin and Robinson returned to Toronto. Anglin then sent Moe a telegram urgently requesting that he get in touch with him. Moe never did and was thrown off the team four days before it left for Mexico. He interpreted this as a sign that the amateur world didn't want him. He had effectively lost his amateur status. He was a "non-amateur."

Moe sent a letter to Anglin in December telling him

that he had decided to turn pro. Anglin said he learned from somebody in Kitchener that Moe had been hiding in an upstairs bedroom in his home when he showed up to speak with him. Moe acknowledged that he sometimes accepted money to help him with expenses for amateur tournaments. "Traveling costs a lot even when you're hitchhiking," Moe said then. "Sure, I took dough to get to places and back, but I paid back most of them after I knew it was dangerous." Wes McKnight, then the president of the Ontario Golf Association, put it this way: "As I understand it, the RCGA dropped him off [the Americas Cup team] because they thought it might embarrass the whole Canadian team if the United States authorities began investigating. There have been a lot of rumors, but I don't think any of them have been proven."

Years later I tried to get to the bottom of the RCGA's interaction with Moe that led to his removal from the Americas Cup team and his loss of amateur status. Marion Doherty tried to help but told me that the files regarding the incident had been lost. Anglin insisted that the matter had been a simple one and that Moe's dismissal from the Americas Cup team had been due to the communication problem, not because the RCGA thought Moe's presence would embarrass the organization or, by extension, Canada. Anglin had repeatedly tried to contact Moe to figure out what was going on, and Moe had ignored him.

After announcing that he would turn professional, prompted by the conflicts surrounding his amateur status violations, Moe finished third in a bursary for Canadian

professionals under thirty and won — or should have won
— $1,500 to play ten weeks on the U.S. winter circuit. But
again he ran aground. The Canadian Professional Golfers'
Association deemed him ineligible to win money because
he held no official status with a club. Who was he? What was
he? The ultraconservative golf world of the 1950s needed
to label Moe. He wasn't a pro, but he wasn't an amateur. He
just wanted to play tournament golf. Moe spent the winter
of 1958 in Florida, but he didn't have the money to play
the winter tour. Upon his return north in the spring, Bert
Turcotte, a Toronto golf pro and club manager who also
ran indoor golf schools in the winter, was looking after De
Haviland and hired Moe. Moe entered the next bursary
tournament and again was one of the three professionals
to win the money to play the winter circuit. He set out to
play ten tournaments on the 1959 U.S. winter tour, against
golfers such as Palmer, Snead, Hogan and Billy Casper —
all major champions.

The American professionals soon let Moe know he
annoyed them. He had come into a world where players
conformed to a set of rules. They were trying to impress
current sponsors and potential sponsors. Moe sometimes
wore the same clothes a few days in a row. His pants were
too short, and his shoes were torn. He stood out: his physical appearance, his sweat-stained visor, his white shirt
blackened on both shoulders from carrying his clubs, his
pants frayed at the bottom, his shoes split open, his speech
patterns, his unusual stance, the swing itself, the speed with
which he played, the fact that he never studied the line of

a putt, and his antics. Moe sometimes hit balls off Coke bottles rather than tees, and when he did use a tee it might be as high as a coffee cup. He used a four-inch tee twice during the 1959 Los Angeles Open.

"I was putting on a show," Moe said. "I was making the crowd laugh." Maybe it was only his nervous energy coming out, but it was impossible not to notice him. Maybe that was helpful to the tour, which, after all, was entertainment as well as a sporting competition. But players and officials didn't see it that way. "They told me it was big business, this was *the* tour of the world, and they didn't care how good I was, I still had to tee it up in the normal way."

His insecurities poured out, but he did play some excellent golf. A story persists that Moe was leading the 1959 Greater New Orleans Open Invitational with seven holes to play, but I couldn't corroborate this claim. Moe was two shots behind leader Bill Collins after three rounds and shot 72 in the last round. He tied for fourth, four shots behind Collins and seven better than Arnold Palmer. Moe won $1,100 and was on the cover of the March 20, 1959, issue of *Golf World*, the U.S. newsweekly of the game. He is shown in two photos. In one, he is setting up to hit a driver, with the ball on a tee so high that the entire wooden clubhead would fit underneath. He's wearing black-and-white striped socks and dark slacks. The other photo shows Moe holding four high tees in his right hand, balancing a ball on each of the two middle tees.

Tour players realized that Moe was a superb ballstriker, a marksman. However, many couldn't get beyond his look and style. In the end, Moe played six PGA Tour events in 1959, making every cut, and returned for the next winter circuit, where he again played six tournaments and finished in the top twenty-five three times. But Moe felt humiliated at one tournament. He showed up at the home that Gus and Audrey Maue had rented in Daytona Beach. Maue was shocked when Moe knocked on his door. He was supposed to be playing in a tournament. Moe told Maue he was finished on the U.S. tour, but he wouldn't say why.

Bert Weaver, an American pro, went to a Daytona Beach club two days later, after the tournament was over. Maue asked him what had happened. "He said that Moe put his ball on a big tee and that he hit it so well. Moe was playing to the gallery, and he was carrying his own bag. A player in his group called Moe aside and told him to fix his teeth and to get new clothes. Moe was insulted and said he'd never play the U.S. tour again."

Many years later I asked Weaver about what had happened. He couldn't recall the details and said only that Moe was "unusual" and that the American pros all liked him once they got to know him.

But it was evident that some players didn't like Moe, which is why he showed up at the Maue home. He never did play again in the United States. The Canadian Open was the only tour event he continued to play. He excelled in Canada, winning two Ontario Opens, three Manitoba Opens, one Saskatchewan Open, three Alberta Opens, two Canadian PGA Championships, and eight Canadian Senior

PGA Championships, including seven in a row. He never won the Canadian Open, but he came close in the country's biggest tournament. That was in 1963, at the Scarboro Golf and Country Club just east of Toronto, when Doug Ford won. Ford had won the 1955 PGA Championship and the 1957 Masters.

I was fifteen years old that summer and went with my dad to the tournament. His store, Superior Automotive Supplies, was a ten-minute drive from the Scarboro course. To me, the course might have been on another planet. I was a year away from driving, but I knew about the course because of its reputation. It had already hosted the 1940, 1947 and 1953 Canadian Opens. Its eighteenth hole played across Scarboro Golf Club Road, and sometimes my father drove me there after work so that we could sit in the car and get glimpses of some member golfers. Later, after I got my driver's license, I delivered auto parts to gas stations as part of my summer job. My father wondered at first why I took so long for what should have been a short drive for a delivery. But he soon accepted that I liked to drive by the Scarboro course and sit in my car to watch some golf. From time to time, I would circle the parking lot so that I could see golfers in their summer clothes on the practice putting green or sitting on the clubhouse veranda sipping a drink after a round. I could have sat in my car for hours watching golf.

I couldn't have guessed, as my dad drove me in his sleek green 1963 Pontiac Parisienne to the Canadian Open at Scarboro, that one day I'd write about Moe and play golf

with him. I was there to watch him in Canada's most significant tournament.

We went out for the first round, which then was played
on a Wednesday. My dad wanted to see George Bayer; he
knew him as Big George Bayer. He was six foot five, and
his hands looked as big as hockey gloves. Bayer had played
six games in the National Football League as a lineman
for the Washington Redskins. He had eventually turned to
professional golf and had won three tour events, including
the 1957 Canadian Open. That Canadian Open was held at
Westmount, where Moe had caddied. He too had played in
the tournament.

Bayer and Moe were alike in some curious ways.
Neither wore a glove. Bayer hardly ever took a practice
swing; Moe never took one. Both used heavy clubs. Moe
liked to say he wanted something that felt like an oak
tree in his hands. But they were also different in important ways. Moe stood to the ball with his feet far apart,
although he was only five foot nine. Bayer stood to the
ball with his feet close together, although he was eight
inches taller. Moe believed in gripping the club so tightly
that he could draw blood, and his hands were full of cal-
luses. Bayer, in contrast, didn't believe in squeezing the
club; he didn't think doing so would provide any more
control and would compromise power. He tended to
spray the ball sometimes, while Moe, with his death grip,
controlled the ball so well. Bayer hit the ball a long way.
Moe was not a long hitter. He was a control player. Bayer
had hit some drives more than 400 yards in competition.

Sports Illustrated in 1961 referred to him as "Golf's Human Howitzer."

My dad, having played some pro football, wanted to see Big George Bayer, the former Redskins player, on the golf course. He'd told me stories of how far Bayer could hit a golf ball. We found Bayer on the sixth hole, a long par-five playing back toward Scarboro Golf Club Road. Bayer had his tee shot far down the fairway and was trying to reach the green.

"Watch this," my dad said as Bayer settled into his three-wood second shot. "He's going to go after it." Bayer took the club back in his languid manner, creating a massive swing arc of some twenty-eight feet. That's six to eight feet longer than the swing arcs of most golfers. He started his downswing in the same, almost slow-motion style and topped the ball about seventy-five yards down the fairway. Bayer was shocked. My dad was shocked. I didn't know what to say.

We followed Bayer for a couple of holes and then sought out Moe, who was playing with fellow Canadian Stan Leonard and Gene Littler. Moe hit the ball cleanly every time. He did make the game look easy, even in the Canadian Open. He shot 71 that first round. I didn't get back to the tournament, but I did follow his progress. He shot 71 in the second and third rounds as well and was in second place with one round to play. Moe had made sixteen bogies and sixteen birdies in the three rounds and was tied with three other golfers, three shots behind Ford. Two photos of Bayer and Moe appeared in the *Toronto Star*, side by side. Bayer was driving, while Moe was hitting a short iron. The headline read, "The Power and the Perfunctory."

Teeder Kennedy was a good friend of Moe's. Kennedy had played for the Toronto Maple Leafs from 1942 to 1957 and had captained the team eight times. He knew something about the qualities it took to win, having been on five Stanley Cup–winning teams with the Leafs. Kennedy tried to convince Moe that he could win the Canadian Open. But Moe wasn't buying it. "I'm a teachin' pro, not a playin' pro," he told his friend. Was Moe setting himself up for a fall?

Ford and Moe played together in the final round. They'd played frequently over the years, starting in the early 1950s at a tournament in Toronto. Moe caught Ford at Scarboro and was leading the tournament into the back nine, but then he started three-putting almost every green. He got twitchy. He had started to think about what he would say at the presentation should he win. The thought unsettled him. This was Canada's biggest tournament. "What was I going to say? I'd be a big man in the country. I'd have to drop the puck at the hockey game."

Forty years later Mike Weir won the Masters. He was the first Canadian male to win a major professional championship. Weir dropped the puck the next day at an NHL playoff game between the Toronto Maple Leafs and the Philadelphia Flyers. He walked the carpet out to center ice wearing the green jacket that goes to the Masters winner. Weir seemed almost shy there. He did interview after interview that day in Toronto. His golf was eloquent that

Sunday at the Augusta National Golf Club, and while he handled the interviews well enough it wasn't natural or easy for him to speak to the country.

Golfers are far more comfortable playing golf than talking about it. They're doers, not speakers. Moe more than anybody struggled with the public side of the game. That part of it wasn't for him. Spectators often bothered him. Sometimes their very presence would disturb him. He was more comfortable at a driving range.

His tetchiness and sensitivity to what was around him helped Ford. Ford hooked his tee shot on the sixteenth hole, and it looked as if the ball was going into the woods. The partisan fans cheered his mistake. Moe reacted. "Moe stood on the tee and read them the riot act," Ford recalled. "I was okay, and then I birdied seventeen and won." Moe shot 75 and tied for twenty-third, eight shots behind Ford. Still, Ford said, "That boy has more talent than any player I've ever seen come out of Canada."

Moe had a faulty memory when it came to that 1963 Canadian Open. After I got to know him, I sometimes accompanied him on his drives along southern Ontario back country roads, and once we drove around Calgary for hours. On one of those drives around Calgary those many years later, I asked him about it. He believed he held a one-shot lead going into the final round. He also said he blew the tournament. "I had six three-putts. I was comfortable from tee to green but not on the greens. It was self-confidence. Not knowing how. Not knowing how to get the ball in the hole. The Canadian Open was controlling me, I wasn't controlling it. It was eating me because I wanted to win it so bad. I'd have had the Grand Slam of Canada, the Canadian Amateur, the CPGA, and the Canadian Open. To this day, I'd still be the talk of Canada."

A bad shot wasn't in my mind. Every time I got over the ball I wondered how good it was going to be. I knew it was going to be good. But how good? — Moe, 1986

MOE'S MIND

I'VE ALWAYS WONDERED WHY even the best golfers sometimes have difficulty taking their practice swings to the golf course. Johnny Miller once told me that the longest walk in golf is from the practice tee to the first tee. Similarly, golfers of all abilities frequently can't make their practice swings on the course their real swings. Something intrudes. Is it the fact that the golfer is trying to make the ball go to the target rather than swinging through blades of grass? My practice swing feels fluid, but my real swing too often deteriorates into a series of positions I'm trying to stitch together. Is the problem mental or psychological? An erratic swing is the manifestation of the difficulty, so golfers — all of us — are prone to believing that the source of the problem is physical. But what if the problem is mental, not mechanical? It's no surprise that tour players work with mental coaches as well as swing coaches. No wonder the literature on the psychology of golf is so extensive that it rivals that of the mechanics of the swing.

Moe was a machine on the practice range and often on the course. But he was more man than machine in that 1963 Canadian Open when he faltered with the title on the line. I've always struggled with taking my practice game to the course and my practice swing to my real swing. My wife, a kind but direct woman who says she doesn't have the self-punishing nature that golf requires, has advised me, more than once, "Just hit it with your practice swing." If only I could. So we enter the realm of the psychology of the game. I don't feel nervous or anxious over the ball on the course, or at least I'm not aware of such feelings. Yet my real swing loops and twists, and I tend to scoop the ball rather than swing through it with my hands leading the clubhead. Miller told me that good players deloft the club through impact, whereas poor players add loft to it. I studied Moe's impact position and noted the extent to which Moe delofted the club; why can't I do that? I had to laugh — I think I did laugh — when I overheard a fellow with whom I'd just played a round at the Mirasol Country Club in Palm Beach Gardens. He'd seen me flail and flip at the ball during the round and said to a friend of mine who had joined us, "That guy played in the British Amateur?" It's true. I did play in the 1977 British Amateur. But I was no longer "that guy." Why? Why? Why? And why couldn't Moe control that 1963 Canadian Open? Why did it control him?

My "Psychology of Golf" file goes back forty years and is more than an inch thick. I'm sure I became a golf writer because I was interested in one fundamental question that I still haven't answered and that I don't believe anybody else has answered satisfactorily. Why is it possible to make a good swing in practice but difficult to take it to the course? Subsidiary questions follow easily. Why can a golfer make a beautiful practice swing on the course but be unable to replicate it on an actual shot? Why can a golfer make a smooth putting stroke just before his real stroke during a round, yet his stroke when it counts turns into a flinch?

Looking through my file, I see that I wrote the following when I was in my early twenties: "I seem to be spending most of my time thinking about golf; it has been my life . . . what am I interested in? To study the volitional processes as they come into play in the golf swing." That is, why can't I, like many golfers, even at the best of times during their careers, make a proper swing when I want to? What happens when the ball is there and the swing matters? Forty years later I am thinking about the same questions. In 2011, as I write, why is Mike Weir, the 2003 Masters champion, having so much trouble taking his game from the practice range to the golf course? Why is Tiger Woods having similar problems? Both Weir and Woods say they can hit the ball well on the range. Well, why can't they do that on the course during a tournament? I've heard all the pat answers. Tournament golf is different from practice or recreational golf; of course it is, but why? What happens to the mind and to the swing? Is the will subservient to the imagination? Why do golfers get the yips putting and on full swings? Hank Haney worked with retired basketball star Charles Barkley in a ten-part series of lessons on the Golf Channel; the objective was to cure the hitch that Barkley had developed in his downswing, when he came to almost a full stop before lurching at the ball. I remember a term from the highly mechanical, even abstruse, approach to the swing called *The Golfing Machine*. It's called "downstroke blackout." Barkley smoothed things out to some degree on the practice range and in his practice swings, but he was the same violent hitcher on his real swings. The series proved only that a golfer isn't always in control of what happens when he makes a swing. Haney couldn't help Barkley, who continues to suffer from his stutter-stop swing. I feel for the guy. He worked with one of the game's top teachers. The project was a total failure.

The problems I mention have been part of golf since the game began hundreds of years ago, and they have interested researchers in fields that at first might seem far removed from the game. Sir Charles Sherrington, the leading neurophysiologist and a student of the nervous system during the last third of the nineteenth century and the first part of the twentieth, was taken with the psychological problems of golf. Sherrington, a professor of physiology at Oxford University from 1913 to 1935, shared the Nobel Prize for Physiology or Medicine in 1932 with Edgar Adrian. He wrote the following in his foreword to *The Brain and Golf:*

Some Hints for Golfers from Modern Mental Science by C.W. Bailey, published in 1923: "The ancient game of golf has a literature of its own; but to relate the raison d'etre of practical maxims for obtaining proficiency with the clubs to underlying principles of physiology and psychology is a venture at once both bold and desirable."

Some golfers thought that mental practice was the key to taking one's game from the practice area to the golf course. In 1915, Jerome Travers, the U.S. Open champion that year, wrote that a golfer must practice concentration: "Most golfers are willing enough to practice physically, but they never think of practicing mentally." One morning I was reading some notes that Lloyd Percival, an innovative trainer in mental and physical practices for athletes, had provided to George Knudson. Percival wanted Knudson to do a brief series of breathing and stretching exercises every morning before getting out of bed, then to perform a few floor exercises, and then to finish "by taking a couple of minutes for Image Practice. Don't use a club but just simulate (eyes shut) a few shots off the tee, with irons and on the green, feeling and imagining yourself stroking the ball perfectly — no tension and complete feel. Concentrate on this — use that imagination to get the feel, see the picture."

Golfers do such imagery training regularly, and yet then sometimes they still play terribly. Weir and Woods and all tour professionals have access to sophisticated training methods meant, with good intentions, to help them in every area of their games. Yet something happens when a golfer is over the ball.

Ernie Els won the 1994 and 1997 U.S. Opens and the 2002 Open Championship (or British Open, as it's known in North America). As he reached his forties, he began to lose his game. His swing still looks smooth and elegant and powerful. But he's been unable to find the game that once seemed as much a part of him as his signature. He said during the summer of 2011, when he missed the cut in the last three majors, that he was "just as low as I've ever been. That's a fact. I've got to get myself through this. I should maybe take some time off and reevaluate everything, see where I'm at. I'm just working hard and not getting anything out of it. I should maybe go away for a while." Els had been working hard to bring a better game to the U.S. Open, the second major of the year. It didn't help; he missed the cut there, in the Open Championship the next month, and then in the PGA Championship. What was going on? Was he trying too hard? Not trying hard enough? Was there too much "corruption of the hard drive" in his approach?

Five-time Open Championship winner Peter Thomson used this term when I asked him what had happened to Nick Faldo after his game started to slip. Faldo had won three Opens and three Masters between 1987 and 1996, but inevitably and inexorably he started to lose form. He changed instructors, lost his feel, and that was that. It wasn't for lack of trying not to try, which is what Dr. Louis Robinson said every golfer has to do to succeed. "It is essential to give one's whole self to each state of the game if anything like success is to be hoped for," Robinson wrote in a December 1897 article called "The Psychology of Golf" in the *North American Review*. "But one must do it in a kind of passive and animal fashion, committing the business as it were to that sub-agent of the will who is in charge of the automatic department. Any attempt to bring the conscious will into play, as one is often tempted to do after a series of exasperating failures, at once sets the automatic department on strike."

Moe put it this way: "Winners play golf automatically. Winners see what they want. Losers see what they don't want. Don't let the game eat you; you eat the game." He defined golf as "hitting an object to a defined target area with the least amount of effort and an alert attitude of indifference." He always said a golfer should "let" himself play, not "make" himself play.

But how does a golfer do that? And is *do* even the right word when the idea is to *let*? Moe had something, but what exactly did he have? And why, after all, couldn't he "let" himself play against the best golfers in the world on the U.S. tour? I dove into the psychology of golf as a young amateur who had his own problems taking his game from the range to the course. I wrote a paper on the subject while pursuing a doctorate in psychology. I started to write about golf professionally and never completed the doctorate. But the file remains, and it has thickened over the years. I have a black binder labeled "Golf Bibliography, 1890–," in which the entries refer to articles on the psychology of golf. There's no year at the end. The subject is endless.

For me, Moe encapsulated many of the issues that I found interesting and had been reading about. He played without affectation, yet his style still set him apart from other golfers, far apart. Everything he did on the course appeared extreme, so much so that it was impossible not to focus on his differences. His stance and swing, the fact that he never took a practice swing or read a putt in any conventional way, these factors alone marked him as somebody who operated in another golfing realm.

His personality also set him apart. Everything about Moe acted as a magnet for spectators to stare at him. His speech patterns, his outlandish clothing choices, the way he often snapped at adults when all they did was say hello. He was so uncomfortable around people he didn't know. Moreover, he often forgot or ignored people he saw regularly.

Neal Mednick, an accomplished Toronto golfer who won the 1971 Eastern Ontario Amateur in Kingston, was about twenty and working the four-to-midnight shift at the CN railway in north Toronto one summer. He went to the nearby Golden Star restaurant for dinner most evenings and noticed Moe sitting alone on the patio. Moe's dinner consisted of a few cheese dogs and Cokes. Neal started to eat with Moe two or three nights during the work week, which added up to some thirty dinners that summer. After the summer ended, Neal went to the Bayview Golf and Country Club for a game with his father and some friends. He saw Moe on the putting green. "I went up and said, 'Hi, Moe, how's it going?' in a familiar tone that made it sound like we knew each other, which I thought we did," Neal told me when we had a game in the summer of 2011. "He turned and said, 'I don't know you, I don't know you.'

The other guys around him looked at me like I was nuts. It was really embarrassing." Neal next ran into Moe at a local driving range, where Moe was hitting balls. Again he said hi to Moe, and again Moe snubbed him. "This was after eating dinner with the guy some thirty-odd times. I remember how much it bugged me, to the point of infuriation. I also remember wanting to say to him, 'What's with you? I've eaten dinner with you at the Golden Star all summer long, and now you behave like you've never even met me. What gives?' I don't know why I didn't, but I didn't. Instead, I just stopped going to the Golden Star."

That was just Moe being Moe, I suppose. But what made him who he was? That question had long become a focal point for me. Did the accident when he was five years old make him the person he was? Was he in fact autistic from birth? I must have thought soon after encountering Moe at De Haviland that he was an automaton, a whirling dervish of the game who, with a golf club in his hands, connected himself to his target and swung away freely. He said, "Be in charge of your thinking." But it didn't seem to me that he "thought" golf. He just whacked a ball around a field to a target. I thought, and continue to think, that he played golf without affectation.

Was his injury the source of his double speaking? Did it have something to do with the extreme shyness and insecurity that he would come to show? Did he suffer any neurological damage? Was the sleigh-ride accident central to the man and the golfer Moe would become? Would he have played golf as he did, so different from the norm, had he not been hit by and dragged under a sedan that mid-January day? Did he indeed suffer frontal lobe damage to his brain, as some of the characteristics he would show suggest? Moe was only five years old. To what degree had his personality, character and traits been formed? If we don't know who he was "before," then it's a tricky business to suggest he was different "after." But maybe he was.

Moe's thought process fascinated not only other critics but me as well, especially after an incident one afternoon when we were playing Maple Downs. Moe seemed lost over a shot on the twelfth tee. The tee shot was blind from where we were playing, so Moe couldn't see his target. It was as if he suddenly had to speak in a different language. He was out of sorts. I told him to aim at a cloud. "Clouds move, clouds move," he said. He was frozen over the ball but finally managed to swing. He hit an indifferent shot. It was as if he were hitting a whiffle ball, not a golf ball. His efficient, tight swing wavered, lost in space.

Shortly after that game, in 1995, I contacted Dr. Richard Keefe, a neuropsychologist at Duke University whose research interests had led him to write about sports and who had a particular interest in golf. His book *On the Sweet Spot* examined the experience of being in the so-called zone, when everything is flowing smoothly and performance comes easily. I sent him some articles I'd written about Moe. He was interested to learn that Moe seemed lost when he couldn't see a target, as was apparent during the round I'd played with him at Maple Downs. Keefe pointed out that one of the symptoms that a person who has suffered a frontal lobe injury exhibits is the inability to hold an image in the mind's eye for more than a second or two. Keefe's particular research interest then was the function of the prefrontal cortex and its central role in working memory. A keen golfer, Keefe believed that Moe's distaste for blind shots in golf could have resulted from the injury Moe had suffered as a child.

"If you think about this type of mental function," Keefe wrote to me about working memory, "you can see how important it is in golf, as golf is one of the only sports in which you do not look at your target. You need to keep all that visual information in working memory. I believe that some of the best players have extraordinary working memory capacities that enable them to maintain a perfect image of the target, the preferred flight of the ball and even the swing they would like to execute."

If Moe had suffered damage to the frontal lobe of his brain, then his difficulty with blind shots would be understandable. So, too, would his fast play. As he said, "One look at the target, and I'm gone." He swung so quickly after looking at the target because his working memory was so limited. Keefe pointed out that patients with frontal lobe damage do very poorly on tests of working memory.

"Moe's social isolation, peculiar behavior and disorganization are typical in people with frontal lobe damage (as well as other conditions)," Keefe wrote. "However, the clincher is that he had particular difficulty with blind shots and putting, which put particularly heavy demands on our abilities to keep visual, especially visuospatial, images in mind, referred to as 'working memory.' This function is mediated by the prefrontal cortex."

A consensus developed over the years that Moe was autistic. The film *Rain Man* had come out in 1988, and many golfers who saw the film thought that they saw Moe in the character of Raymond Babbitt, played by Dustin Hoffman. But was Moe autistic? If he was, to what degree? Babbitt can't do much on his own. He needs assistance all the time. This wasn't true of Moe. He drove himself to Florida every winter. He did take the same route every year and stayed in the same motels: he needed routine. But many Canadian snowbirds did the same. Moe was inflexible in his ways, but he was functioning on his own, unlike Rain Man. He even lived on his own.

Keefe didn't think Moe was autistic. "People with autism have severely disturbed early years, which doesn't seem to be the case with him," he wrote. He also mentioned that, if Moe had suffered a brain injury, it had probably happened long ago. That was, of course, the case. He wrote that, in all likelihood, Moe would have adopted some alternative strategies to cope. For Moe, I think, golf was the main strategy.

Still, Moe was very different from others. There was no doubt about that. Barry Morrow wrote *Rain Man* and received an Academy Award for Best Original Screenplay. Morrow had only recently taken up golf when he read the cover story about Moe that David Owen had written in *Golf Digest's* December 1995 issue. The twenty-page article brought Moe to the attention of golfers around the world.

Morrow immediately saw the cinematic possibilities in his story and decided that he wanted to do a film about Moe and to write the script. Morrow told me he viewed the tale "as a story about an underdog character you want to see protected against the slings and arrows of life." He wrote to Moe in July 1997, care of the Canadian Professional Golfers' Association, hoping the letter would reach him. "I read about you in *Golf Digest*," Morrow wrote, "and marveled at your journey as a person and golf legend."

The letter reached Moe, and a visit was arranged. Morrow traveled to Kitchener from his home in Santa Barbara. He and Gus Maue met Moe at the motel room in Kitchener where he lived. Moe answered the door wearing boxer shorts and an undershirt and holding a three-wood. They chatted for a short time. Moe called Morrow a "knucklehead," which meant he liked him. They met again over the next few days. Morrow also met Nick Weslock. An agreement was eventually struck. Morrow started to write the script and to look for financing.

It appeared that the film would get made on a small budget with an independent producer. Morrow's script focused on the 1950s, when Moe made it to the PGA Tour for two years. He was in Arnold Palmer's world, and he didn't feel comfortable there. Morrow wanted to show how Moe coped and to suggest that golf was indeed a vehicle for him to express himself. He knew Moe was somehow able to make a life for himself in golf even though he didn't feel comfortable with the public side of the game. What was it in him that allowed him to function and even to thrive?

Morrow's script looked at this question. Morrow set the film in the 1950s, when Palmer was drawing support because of his bold play and President Dwight D. Eisenhower was helping to popularize the game because he liked it and played frequently. This was also the dawn of the television age and of tournament coverage. Palmer was telegenic. He fit. Moe didn't.

In the winter of 2009, four and a half years after Moe died, I met Barry Morrow in Santa Barbara. I didn't have my clubs or golf shoes with me, but he provided me with both. The shoes had once belonged to Moe, who had given them to Barry. Later we joined our wives for dinner, where we spoke about what made Moe such a compelling figure that Barry would want to do a film about him. Barry told me that he wanted to do a "poem" about Moe, meaning that the film wouldn't be a biography of the man. It would reflect the struggles of a gifted, unusual man playing a game whose major figures effectively shunned him. But Moe kept at his craft. Against all odds, he made a satisfying life for himself.

Morrow wasn't the only person who thought Moe might have been autistic. Dr. Tom Saunders, a Calgary physician, had written me a letter in December 1994 on stationery marked "Mind-Body Golf." Saunders, then in his early seventies, was an accomplished gentleman. He had flown reconnaissance missions over the North Sea from 1940 to 1943 with the Royal Canadian Air Force and later graduated from medical school at McGill University. He had been a founding member of the University of Calgary's Faculty of Medicine and chief of staff for three years at the former Holy Cross Hospital in the city. He had returned to university and at the age of fifty-five had received a master's degree in medical education from Michigan State University. Saunders had traveled far beyond Calgary since he'd been the director of postgraduate training for seven years for rural physicians in Nepal. After he retired in 1986, he pursued with relish his interest in golf. At the same time, he was intrigued by the role that the mind played in golf and particularly in mental practice via hypnosis. He went on to self-publish a book, *Golf: The Mind-Body Connection*, accompanied by two CDs that included exercises for mental practice.

Saunders was aware of Moe and had read Donna Williams' memoir *Nobody Nowhere: The Extraordinary Story of an Autistic Girl*. The book, he told me in his letter, was "the sad story of an autistic person and her struggle to be accepted by the world." He found her story inspirational in that she was on her way to completing a doctorate. Williams, an Australian, has since gone on to write three more books. She speaks around the world about the autism spectrum — the range of behavior associated with the condition. She was severely abused as an infant and misdiagnosed frequently before being considered autistic.

Saunders recognized that it's always dangerous to make long-distance diagnoses but thought that Williams described some behaviors that he'd seen in Moe, his extraordinary shyness, for one. He also pointed to Moe's repetitive thoughts and speech and his knowledge of how many balls he'd hit in practice.

"The link I made was: what if Moe is autistic?" Saunders wrote in his letter. "What a wonderful story of his accomplishments over such adversity. How sad that we as a society have so much difficulty with out of the ordinary behaviors. Of course the problem is how to find out. How would Moe feel about having a label? How could a diagnostic workup be organized, and who is a trusted friend who can win his confidence to achieve this? And who would he trust his innermost thoughts to?"

After hearing from Saunders — who died in June 2008 — I thought a lot about what he suggested and decided to talk to Dr. Keefe again to see whether he still thought Moe's behavior was caused by the frontal lobe injury given the new discoveries being made about autism. In 1995, I asked him if he would diagnose Moe. This would depend, of course, on whether I could gain Moe's confidence and agreement. I said I'd take Moe to the Mount Sinai School of Medicine in the Bronx, where Keefe was then an assistant professor of psychiatry. He offered to do the diagnosis, which would involve at least a one-hour interview and possibly a series of neuropsychological tests that could take between two and five hours.

Over the years, I had wondered whether it would be helpful in understanding Moe to have him undergo neurological testing. After speaking with Keefe, I told Moe that many people were interested in him and that the scientific world might learn something if he were tested. After all, as unusual as he was, he'd made a life for himself in golf. He thought it was a good life. There was at the same time a sadness about Moe because he never got over the feeling that people were laughing at him, yet he was doing exactly what he wanted to do, all the time.

"The last thing I say in bed every night is 'I wonder how many people said my name today,'" Moe had told me when he was in his late fifties. "Even in countries where I've never been, they've heard of this guy Moe Norman. 'He can hit the ball so straight.' I can control my destiny from tee to green. I did it for thirty-five years, and I'm still doing it. So how can I feel bad? Not when I got something everybody in the world wants. No sirree, I feel good, I feel good."

Moe agreed to be tested as long as I and Nick Weslock would accompany him. But, in the end, I decided not to proceed with the diagnosis. I couldn't overcome the feeling that I was turning Moe into a lab rat, and I wondered what really would be gained from having Moe tested. Why would it matter if he were labeled with a neurological condition?

In 2001, I collaborated with filmmakers Michael Savoie and Anne Pick to do a one-hour documentary on Moe called *The King of Swing* for CBC's Life and Times series. We filmed Moe on the playing field near his boyhood home, where he hit balls. He showed us where he'd buried his golf clubs in front of his home because he'd thought his father didn't approve of him playing golf and didn't want them in the house. We filmed Moe in his motel room and at golf clubs where he felt comfortable. We spoke with his boy-hood chums. One scene in particular lodged in my mind and remains there. Moe was playing cards with some of his friends. At one point, he started to talk about his father in a sneering voice. I shuddered. Had he carried this bitterness with him all his life? There were so many questions about Moe. They only intensified for me after his death.

In 2011, I decided to follow up with Dr. Keefe again; this time I wouldn't be subjecting Moe to any laboratory experiments, but perhaps I could provide Keefe with enough evidence that he could give me a qualified diagnosis. I asked him if he would view the CBC documentary and offer a diagnosis of Moe based on what he saw. I realized this would be his opinion and his opinion only, not the same as a diagnosis based on testing. But maybe I'd learn more about Moe.

Keefe reviewed the tape and got back to me quickly. He sent me a list of Moe's behaviors that he'd noticed along with some accompanying questions. He observed that Moe talked only about golf, nothing else; that he said everything two or three times; that he didn't understand the social context of a situation; that there was a noticeable injury to the left side of his face (but did his odd behavior really start after the accident?); that he didn't look people in the eye; that he didn't say goodbye to people when leaving them; that he became a big fan of self-help tapes, which seem to have helped him; and that he'd said, "I tell my little robot what I think."

"I am becoming increasingly convinced that Moe had Asperger's syndrome," Keefe told me. "It is in the spectrum of autism but has some of the specific features that Moe demonstrated. With many of these brain disorders, it is not a black-and-white thing but has many shades of gray because of the complexity of how our genes interact with the rest of us, including complex personal histories, culture and other genes. The accident he had could have exacerbated the expression of his Asperger's, or it also could have been (as we see all the time with schizophrenia) that family members attempt to point to a specific event as a catalyst."

Symptoms of Asperger's can include repetitive speech patterns and an intense focus on one area with little interest in other areas. It was impossible, for example, to imagine Moe reading a paper or watching a news show. Somebody with Asperger's might also demonstrate repetitive motor mannerisms, which Moe certainly exhibited; his golf swing was the most obvious example. There was also the symptom known as "walking dictionary syndrome," in which the person will come up with a non-stop flood of words about his obsession. Moe's golf talk was usually a torrent. Once Moe started, he kept going and going. I was at events where he got locked into a ritualized speech, almost as if his brain had settled into a groove from which he couldn't escape until he exhausted himself. His speeches were frequently broken records, a needle stuck in an old, long-playing record. If you heard him speak once at a function, well, you'd likely hear the same speech the next time.

People with Asperger's are typically inappropriate in social situations. They get locked into ways of behaving that allow them to feel in control but that surprise other people or make them feel uneasy. It's a reflexive but inaccurate step to believe that a person with Asperger's is being mean. I thought of that moment in the CBC film when Moe got up from the card table and walked out of the room, sputtering bitterly about his father. I also thought, and continue to think, that Moe wasn't mean. He was alone, utterly alone, except for golf, his friend — and his tormentor — for life.

THAT SWING

THE GOLF SWING HAS BEEN the subject of study, debate, argument, conjecture and confusion since the game started some four centuries ago. Newton's Third Law of Motion states that for every action there is an equal and opposite reaction. The first law of swing analysis could be stated as this: "For every swing thought, there is an equal and opposite swing thought." Jack Nicklaus stated that a steady head is the bedrock of the swing. Jack Grout, his swing coach since Nicklaus was ten years old, held the youngster's head by his hair to ingrain that fundamental in the prodigy. Nicklaus did rather well, winning eighteen major championships during his professional career. He was thirty-eight when *Golf Magazine* published an article in the

November 1978 issue demonstrating that tour pros move their heads rotationally, laterally and vertically during their swings. Swing sequence photos of more than 100 players demonstrated his point. But Nicklaus thought that he kept his head rock steady. In golf, however, as even the most respected instructors often say, feel is rarely real.

Many people have studied Moe's swing closely to try to ascertain why it held up so well, even as Moe reached his seventies. The art of the game is to control the flight of the ball, and Moe did that all his life. Of course, he hit 800 balls a day for forty years, but other golfers have hit hundreds of balls a day for years and never developed a repetitive, reliable swing.

Moe wasn't a power golfer in the sense of hitting the ball a long way. There was power in his game, however, and it was in his control. That's why visitors to De Haviland stopped practicing when he hit balls. That's why PGA Tour pros suspended their practices during the Canadian Open when he meandered onto the range.

Deviations in a golf swing normally occur during the swing itself, which is why it's easy to distinguish one player from another from 100 yards away. Most players, however, address the ball in similar ways. Sure, some are more open or closed, but they all stand about the same distance from the ball. They spread their feet apart about the same width. Their knees are bent at about the same angle. Their hands and arms hang from their shoulders in similar manners.

Moe varied noticeably from the conventional, right from the start. His feet were farther apart than those of most players, and he separated them more as he got older. He stretched his arms out from his body as far as possible and set his hands much higher than is customary. There was no bend in his elbows; every other golfer bends the elbows to some extent. Moe set his clubhead nearly a foot behind the ball rather than directly behind it. I've never seen another golfer place his clubhead more than an inch behind the ball at address.

These variations alone distinguished Moe from every other golfer. He wasn't merely outside the box; he was outside the arena. Collectively, his variations formed his signature as he stood over the ball. Yet he didn't arrive at these positions by thinking about them. It's not as if he sat down and reflected on which positions at address would help him to achieve an efficient swing with the least margin of error possible. It's not as if he discussed the matter with a swing coach. Lloyd Tucker, his teacher at Rockway, encouraged Moe to stand to the ball the way he wanted. If the ball flew properly, what else mattered? "He developed his own swing through trial and error," Tucker once said. "Then he built his own truly unique style through hours and hours of repetition." Studied in hindsight, the variations in Moe's swing make common sense. They make so much common sense that, over the course of my golfing life, while following the best players, I've wondered why every golfer doesn't swing the club like Moe did.

A golfer needs a solid base. Why, then, not set one's feet well apart? The wider the separation, the more stable the position, up to a point. That point is beyond where golfers customarily arrange their feet.

It's advantageous to swing with one's arms extended because doing so minimizes a source of error. The golfer who sets up with arms fully extended needs only to maintain that position to achieve uniformity during the swing. The arms won't collapse or stretch farther. The golfer who sets up with arms bent at the elbows creates a potential source of error. If the arms straighten during the swing, he'll need to return them to the starting position to get to the ball properly.

Moe set himself up for maximum extension, promoting a wide and efficient swing arc from the start. His setup helped to create a swing engineered for accuracy. Placement of the clubhead behind the ball further contributed to his chances of hitting an accurate shot. Instructors have long advocated that a golfer should swing the clubhead back low to the ground. Picking up the club abruptly creates a potential source of error while restricting the width and length of the arc. The first three feet of the swing are crucial. Moe instinctively sensed this. He set up with his clubhead already low to the ground; he effectively started his backswing before he moved the clubhead. He didn't need to swing the clubhead low for that first foot; he was already there. He was swinging before he swung.

Why did Moe set up in such a radical, if sensible, way? He didn't know, certainly not at first. His setup felt right to him, and the ball flight told him all he needed to know about its efficacy. Unstudied, it worked. Moe was fortunate that Tucker didn't try to unspool his swing and analyze it or change his unique motion. Tucker encouraged Moe to find his own way, and his way was unlike anybody else's. Nobody stood to the ball like he did. He was rigid, but, he said, "It felt good to me, so I stuck to it. All my boy friends told me I'd never be any good, but I stuck to it. Once I did it, it made sense to me."

But Moe didn't hit the ball initially with anything like the control he eventually developed. That was due in part to using clubs that weren't right for him. He hit duck hooks all the time, "the worst duck hook you ever saw from when I was fourteen until I was eighteen," he told me. Tucker saw the problem with Moe's clubs. "He told me that, if I liked standing the way I did, and he could see that I could move from there, he would get me a set of clubs. I looked like a Jehovah's Witness over the ball, but once I moved, oh, the fluidity."

Tucker did advise Moe to strengthen his hands by squeezing a tennis ball. His hand strength helped him to hit those 800 balls a day, and sometimes more, for years. The count added up to millions during his life. He knew the running total because he counted the number every day.

Tucker also wanted Moe to narrow his stance when he saw how wide apart Moe liked to place his feet. But, Tucker said, "He was stubborn. He had his feet so far apart he was immobilizing his lower body, but he was able to turn. He wouldn't change unless he found it was better for him, and with all the practicing he did he never found it to be useful to change his stance. Once he'd played enough to develop habits, he was reluctant to make any changes."

Moe had a choke hold on the club every time he made

a swing; I was playing with him once when he showed me the palms of his hands and told me they wouldn't hurt even if I scratched them. His fingers and palms were the consistency of sandpaper. To grasp his palm was to hold a plank of wood. Dissecting his swing frame by frame via video analysis at an early stage wouldn't have been of value to Moe. What would a view of his swing's details have achieved, for him, that is, not for the golf world? He found a way to swing, and so he did. We, not Moe, wanted to understand the factors that contributed to his efficiency and repetitiveness. We craved the reliability of his swing. He had it. He didn't need to look for it or to understand its origins or specifics. Moe came to know why his swing worked, and to be able to speak about it at clinics and dinners, but this was long after it had become his signature.

Moe didn't always apply a death grip to his clubs. Once, while playing with him, I noticed that he was aiming for the corner of the fairway, but he missed. I wasn't really shocked given that he was playing with a tiny margin of error. He wanted to drive down the right side on the par-five as close to the rough as possible, the better to open up the green from there so that he could go at it on his second shot. His position was also interesting because his ball settled down into the rough; only half the ball was visible, even if it was but a yard off the fairway. What would Moe do?

He walked into the rough, looked at his lie and took out his four-wood. He gripped the club without much pressure at all, lightly, in fact. I wondered at this. Moe always advocated gripping the club with extreme pressure, especially in his left hand. The thick rough could grab his clubhead and twist it as he came through the ball, so it seemed reasonable that he would hold the club fiercely. Instead, he gripped it so lightly, as if he were holding a butterfly. Then he swung it with what appeared to be no effort at all. I thought of what the great Canadian amateur Marlene Streit advises for every swing: smoothness, rhythm and balance. The ball popped out of the rough easily. It flew straight for the right side of the green and then turned slightly to the left before rolling up thirty feet from the hole. Moe had that putt for an opening eagle. But what had impressed me was the ease with which he'd swung. He hadn't extricated the ball from the rough; he'd merely caressed it out of there, caressed it with power.

Moe was sixty then and still swinging with effortless power. After turning fifty in 1979, he had won the next seven Canadian PGA Senior Championships. He won again in 1987, eight wins in nine years. Clearly, his swing was efficient. I thought it was also graceful.

"You have to use smooth centrifugal force in this game," Moe said as we walked up the fairway toward the green. "Everybody uses brute force, not smooth force. I swung way easier on that shot. Everybody else swings harder."

Moe stayed with what felt good to him. He hadn't read a golf book. He never did read an instruction book, as far as I know. Why would he have? Meanwhile, Moe had a knack for accuracy in other sports. He'd hit .610 in that softball league as a youngster. He also used to stop by St. Jerome's High School to watch football games and often asked Hap

Shantz, the referee, for the ball. Moe liked to stand at the forty-five-yard line and drop-kick field goals. He kicked the football through the uprights time after time.

For Moe, swinging the golf club was another way he could exert control. It made him feel good to be able to control the flight of the golf ball. He gave up other sports after taking up golf and soon identified himself as a golfer and a golfer only. He played amateur tournaments all over southern Ontario, and nobody could touch him. It was as if he were connected to his club, his club was connected and then glued to the ball, and the ball was tied to the target. Moe was a package: mind, body, club, ball, target. The physical act of propelling a golf ball toward a target came easily to him.

At the same time, golf is a mental game. Moe had excelled in reaction sports such as baseball and hockey. How could he cope with how long it took to play golf and the fact that he had to initiate the swing? He wasn't reacting. He was acting. He was creating, not reacting. Golf is mentally daunting because the ball just sits there. A golfer has to find a way to start the swing; there's nothing to react to because nobody is throwing or shooting an object to the golfer. Golf lacks an ignition switch, so the player must supply it. But how does one ignite an action when the object is stationary?

Moe arrived at a novel solution, although it's not accurate to suggest he thought about how to turn golf into a game in which it felt as if somebody were actually throwing something at him so that he needed to react. Somehow he thought the target was coming at him, as if it were a projectile, and the only way for him to defend himself was to propel himself — his whole self — back toward it. The target flowed into him, and then his instincts took over and guided him. In this way, Moe was a passive golfer. He obeyed his instincts. He had no choice in the matter. He played golf without thought.

Moe converted golf into a target game. He wasn't hitting a ball, nor was he reacting to a stationary object. He ignited his swing by turning his head to the left and locking onto the target. He saw the target, he internalized it and he felt the swing he needed to make. He felt it deeply. He became the swing he was about to make, and he sensed that he had to make it immediately. Had he waited, he'd have lost the target he'd grabbed onto. He reacted to his target.

Moe called himself the "747 of golf. One look and I swing, one look and I swing." He never took a practice swing in his life, at least not over the ball. That was wasteful. It also introduced an element of time into the game. A practice swing over the ball would interrupt the circuits that he set in motion when he locked onto the target. He played by surrending himself to the target. To stand there and take a practice swing meant he would lose the target and add time to an already slow game. Moe played outside time because he took no time. He thereby neutralized the psychological complexities of the game, all part of turning it into a reaction sport.

●

IN THE SUMMER OF 1996, WHILE working on an article about
Moe, I asked teaching professional Craig Shankland to analyze Moe's swing in order to suggest what the average player
could learn from it. Shankland was from serious sporting
stock. His father, Bill, had been a top swimmer, cricketer,
boxer and rugby player in Australia. He was touring for
its national rugby team in England when he decided to
remain there. Shankland finished second once and third
twice in the British Open, and he never missed a cut in the
years he played the championship, between 1937 and 1955.
His hands were so strong that he could spread his fingers,
place a beer cap between them and bend the metal. Craig's
mother, from New Zealand, was a classical pianist. Craig,
then in his mid-fifties, was born in England. Asked about
the key to playing good golf, he often invokes the acronym
NATO, "never attach to outcomes." He also believes that golf
is the ultimate individual game and that the wise instructor
doesn't try to coach out a player's idiosyncrasies.

Craig had known Moe for a few years, and they had
become close friends. They met when Moe watched him
conduct a free clinic. Shankland concluded what he thought
was a perfect display of shot making, and Moe came up and
asked him if he knew who he was. Shankland said he did.
Moe then asked if he could come in the next week and
show Shankland the proper way to hit a ball. Shankland invited him to come by, and that was the start of what would
turn into eighteen years of doing clinics together. The man
who could multiply numbers rapidly told Shankland that
41,352 people had attended their clinics. Moe told him that

he'd counted every person who had attended every clinic, how many balls they'd hit and how many tees they'd used.

Craig told me that everything in Moe's swing was based on his setup. Following is Shankland's complete analysis of Moe's swing.

Notice Moe's hands at address. He keeps them high and relatively far from his trunk. This is a beautiful thing to see. The hands are high, and Moe seems to be reaching for the ball. But he is merely extending himself so that he can ensure a constant arc during his swing. The golfer who keeps his hands closer to the ball increases the likelihood that he will be pulled forward by the centrifugal force in the swing. Moe sets up for maximum extension and then stays in this powerful position.

You will also notice that Moe's hands are high at address; his arms run into the shaft. There's no break or angle. The player who sets up with an angle here is likely to find himself in a weak position at impact. The player who appears loose and sloppy at address, and whose hands hang like a rope, won't be solid at impact, when the clubface crashes into the ball at high speed. That's where you must be solid.

BALL POSITION

Moe plays the ball off his left heel because he's thinking of tearing through it and down the target line. The most noticeable element in the relationship of his body to the ball at address is how far behind the ball he places his hands. He puts the clubhead fourteen inches behind the ball, which accomplishes four very good things that any golfer, with practice, will find useful.

(1) The first foot of the backswing is eliminated. Moe is already into his backswing, even before he's started it. He can't take the club back outside, because his right shoulder is already into his backswing. He's already behind the ball.
(2) The clubhead placement prevents Moe from lifting the club as the first move in his backswing. The clubhead is more than a foot behind the ball and still low to the ground.
(3) This encourages a wide arc. Moe is already into his turn, and the width he has set up at address eliminates the possibility of his swaying away from the ball.
(4) The placement of the club relative to the ball, by eliminating the possibility of Moe lifting the club, also prevents a steep plane. The placement promotes the club moving back, not up.

Also observe Moe's head position, well behind the ball. His ball position puts him behind the ball and on his right side at address. Every golfer wants to move to his right, or rear, side during the swing. Moe is there at address and keeps himself there during his backswing.

BACKSWING

Moe's address means that he'll take the club back with his hands, arms and shoulders. Everything else is still. Moe's feet are flat as he sweeps the club away and feels he's keeping his hands in front of his body. He does make a natural turn behind the ball, but the sensation he has is of moving the clubhead back in a straight line from the ball. There's no twisting or intended or manipulated rotation. Moe knows where the clubhead is, and it helps that he uses heavy clubs. A player needs to know where the club-head is. It's easier to know where it is when the player can feel the clubhead.

Note my comment that there's no "intended or ma-nipulated rotation." There's rotation, all right, but it's created only because Moe sweeps the clubhead away from the ball. Everything below is quiet. Moe sweeps the club away and rotates his upper body around his fixed center. There's very little hip rotation but plenty of shoulder rotation. Moe stretches fully as he winds up and creates torque.

Moe's backswing plane is perfect. His club is behind him, rather than above — a Ferris wheel or merry-go-round image. It's behind his right shoulder rather than above his head.

DOWNSWING

Moe begins his downswing with a move of his left knee forward, still keeping his feet flat on the ground. His arms drop into the "slot," all of twenty-one inches, as Moe says. His knees separate as his left knee moves forward. He ap-pears to be squatting slightly to the ball, as Sam Snead did. At the same time, he has created clubhead lag.

Impact

Here Moe pours it on. His feet are still flat on the ground, his left hand is ready to take the hit, and his right hand is steaming through to provide the hit. Moe creates an extremely long "flat spot" at the bottom of his swing. Moe feels his hands are still square to the target twenty-two inches past the ball; the image is stored so clearly in his mind's eye and helps him lead the clubhead through the ball and along that flat spot and on the target line. Moe's hands really aren't square to the target twenty-two inches past the ball, but the image he has of doing this promotes his move through the ball and generates his accuracy. It's one reason he hits the ball so straight. As he says, "If they had a tournament at midnight, I'd be the only one who could find my ball. I'd know where to walk, right down the middle."

Follow-Through and Finish

Moe is consistent through the ball, consistent with what went before and what he was thinking about even before he started his swing. He is keeping his feet on the ground as long as possible, thereby ensuring the clubhead will travel as far along the line as possible and not turn over. Moe wants the sensation of the ball on the clubhead all the way through impact. His feet roll, but they do not lift. His right foot stays down flat until well into the follow-through. The club pulls him with it. His balance is superb due to the security his wide stance produces.

Moe's club does not go behind him after impact, as

happens in most every player's swing. It remains in front of him, and he finishes with his hands reaching for the sky. His finish is a by-product of his feeling of extension and of his not wanting to swing around his body. "Swing through the course, not around it," Moe says.

There is a distinct upper body "lean" at the end of Moe's swing. He doesn't lean backward or create a reverse C shape. The upper body must move forward, or he would get stuck on his right side because of his wide stance. Moe's body is straight over his left shoe at the finish.

Moe plays straight-line golf better than anybody: he swings through the course. That's why he walks a straight line hole after hole. No golfer walks a straighter line. By practicing and learning to adopt some or all of Moe's ideas, you too can walk a straighter line. Moe shows that golf really can be a game of straight lines.

●

MOE USED THICK RUBBER GRIPS to promote quiet hands throughout the swing — "Fingers are fast, fingers are fast, palms are calm, palms are calm," he said. His view was that a person doesn't hold a hammer in his fingers when striking a nail, so why would somebody hold a club in his fingers when striking a golf ball? Why not let the club ride high in the palms rather than the fingers? Why overlap the little finger of the bottom hand between the index finger and middle finger of the top hand, as the majority of golfers do? Why interlock that finger between the index finger and middle finger as a minority of golfers, including Jack Nicklaus and Tiger Woods, did? A ten-finger or baseball grip came to make sense to Moe, although this was a late development. Not until he was about sixty did he change to a ten-finger grip from a conventional grip in which he set the little finger of his right hand between the index and middle fingers of his left hand. Photographs and swing sequences clearly show that Moe used this overlapping grip when he won his tournaments.

Canadian professional golfer Ken Tarling conducted many clinics with Moe at the Royal Oak course in Titusville, Florida. The Canadian PGA used to own the course, and Moe frequently visited there during his winters in Florida. One day Tarling noticed that Moe was using a ten-finger grip. He asked why. Moe was by then representing the company Natural Golf, which was paying him a sizable annual stipend to promote its clubs and instructional approach. The founder, Jack Kuykendall, a Chicago businessman who had studied physics in college and was an avid golfer, had decided at age forty-four to spend six years trying to lower his twelve handicap. But after two years of lessons, his handicap had gone up, not down. It was fourteen after two years of lessons, so Kuykendall decided to figure things out on his own. He studied the swing and settled on a particular method that, he concluded, was the most mechanically efficient possible.

Mark Evershed, a Canadian teaching professional, had been doing some clinics in California when a colleague invited him to visit Kuykendall because he thought

Evershed would be interested in his ideas. Evershed told me that Kuykendall gave him some notes — Evershed called them a "makeshift book" — and a putter whose grip forced the player into an unusual grip. Evershed went to a driving range at a local club, read what Kuykendall had given him and thought, "This is Moe." He told Kuykendall this. "What's a Moe Norman?" Kuykendall asked him. He wasn't aware of Moe. Evershed sent him a copy of a profile of Moe that CBC had aired on its *Fifth Estate* program and for which the host, Bob McKeown, had interviewed me. Kuykendall viewed Moe's swing and saw that it exhibited perfect mechanics. He realized that Moe's swing was eerily similar to the approach he'd come up with independently, so he tried to contact Moe. It took Kuykendall two years to set up a meeting with Moe. They finally met in December 1992 at Royal Oak. Kuykendall explained to Moe why, in his opinion, he was indeed the best ball-striker in the world.

"Moe went to the trunk of his car and pulled out these black-and-white photos of his swing from 1963 and said, 'All my life I've wondered why I'm the greatest ball-striker,'" Kuykendall told me when I spoke with him in the summer of 2011. "He threw the photos on the table and said, 'Take them.' I said I couldn't take them, but he said I could. 'If I can help people, take them.' So I did." They then hit balls on the range and had lunch. On March 13, 1994, Moe signed an agreement with Kuykendall's Natural Golf Corporation that allowed the company to make commercial use of video footage of Moe that had been shot a week earlier. Moe was to receive five percent of the wholesale price of the videos sold. Then, on August 10, 1994, Moe signed a contract with Natural Golf that included a signing bonus of $2,000 and a ten percent royalty on videos, books and clubs the company would manufacture. This would be a Moe Norman signature line of clubs. Moe was to be paid fifty cents U.S. for each iron and wood sold. He would be paid $800 for every one-hour clinic Natural Golf scheduled for him under its auspices. He was guaranteed $27,000 U.S. annually for the three years of the contract. Kuykendall and Moe, in the presence of his attorney, signed the contract.

I was invited to attend a meeting in early June 1995 at the Venture Inn, a Burlington, Ontario, hotel. Kuykendall was there. So were Moe, his lawyer and Nick Weslock. "Moe is the best-kept secret in golf," Kuykendall said, and spoke about producing a fireside chat with Moe that "would show Moe for the genius he is, not the clown that he is." Kuykendall said that, while he thought Moe's swing was just about mechanically perfect, he didn't believe that the overlapping grip was ideal. He said it compromised the "single-axis swing" that was the most mechanically efficient. In such a swing, the golfer takes the club back on one path and returns it to the ball on the same path. Moe had always tried to swing the club that way, and, he said, "I was the first guy to come out with my right-hand grip thicker than the left, so the club couldn't turn over." His grip was built up thicker toward the bottom to better enable this approach. Still, Kuykendall thought, Moe could shift his grip even more toward the ideal if he put all his fingers on the club while letting it sit as much in his palms as possible.

Moe was holding a putter while Kuykendall spoke and appeared almost to go into a trance. "What have I got to lose, a lousy golf ball?" Moe asked. "People are afraid of success. I want to, not I got to, I want to shoot sixty-five, not I got to shoot sixty-five." Moe was speaking quickly. "I'm sixty-five, and I've never been through a doctor's door because I get along with myself. A missed golf shot will never hurt my golf swing, only my vanity, and vanity is the luxury of fools. How true, how true. Golf is work without toil, intoxication without the hangover."

Moe talked about grip pressure and said that he wanted to draw blood from the last three fingers of his left hand. This sat well with Kuykendall. "The reason is we don't want the left hand to move. You want to tighten the tendons so that your wrist won't twist."

Moe always gripped the club tightly, and it always rode high in his right and left palms, so much so that he often had cuts in the heel pad of his left hand. Tarling says Moe wanted the back of his left hand to feel like an extension of the club, so he let the shaft ride high there rather than sit in the fingers — where most golfers have it. Moe's grip had always been more of a palm than a finger grip, even if he had used the overlapping style before meeting Kuykendall. When I asked Moe why he switched to the ten-finger grip, he told me that Kuykendall said it was the right way and that he needed the money. Kuykendall told me that Moe asked him if he could recommend anything that would make him even better than he was. "I told Moe that if he separates his hands, rather than overlapping them, he'll have better control. He used the ten-finger grip the rest of his life." He used it because Kuykendall advised him to do so. Nothing in the contract, which I have, stipulates this as a condition of the agreement with Natural Golf. To me, the change that Moe made in something so fundamental as his grip, after winning so many tournaments with a standard grip, is further evidence of his deep insecurity. Nearly forty years after he ripped up his left thumb because he hit so many balls at the Masters following the advice of Sam Snead, he effectively ripped up the grip he'd used all his life.

•

ON THE SUNDAY BEFORE THE WEEK of the 2011 Masters, I drove up from Jupiter, Florida, to see Craig Shankland at the LPGA International Golf Club in Daytona Beach, where he was teaching. We'd been in touch over the years, and I wanted to spend some time with him to see how he felt about Moe six and a half years after his death. Craig was driving back to Daytona from Aspen on September 4, 2004, when he got the news of Moe's death. He had to pull over to the side of the road to compose himself.

Craig was working with Bud Cauley, a University of Alabama junior who would go on to qualify for the 2011 U.S. Open. Cauley decided to forgo his senior year and turn pro at the U.S. Open. He'd been home-schooled before going to Alabama, which fit with Craig's views of allowing a person to figure things out for himself or at least not as part of a group. Cauley went on to win enough money in eight starts on the 2011 PGA Tour to qualify for the 2012 season there without going through qualifying school. He was only the sixth golfer ever to accomplish that.

By the time I sat down with Craig, more than sixty years had passed since Moe first met Lloyd Tucker at the Rockway Golf Club. Tucker and Craig shared the view that golf must be taught one to one. It is indeed, as Tom Kite once put it, the "onliest" game. "I've always loved quirky swings that work," Craig told me as we ordered lunch. "We need these players. It's necessary to allow individuality. I think we're over-instructing players. If somebody has an innate ability to put the club on the ball, why would you want to take that away? What have you got then? I looked at Moe, and I said how good it is, not how stupid it is. Look at Jack Nicklaus. He lifted his left heel off the ground, and his right elbow flew in his backswing. Christy O'Connor let go of the club at the top of his swing and then regripped it and flung it at the ball. Or look at Jim Furyk."

Nicklaus has won more major championships than any golfer. The Irish player Christy O'Connor played in ten Ryder Cups from 1955 to 1973 and won six Senior PGA Championships in Europe. Furyk loops the club on his backswing but gets it back on the ball, which is all that matters. He won the 2003 U.S. Open.

Why, then, would Moe ever want to change? He trapped his swing, and it sent the ball exactly where he wanted it to go, shot after shot after shot. Craig once asked Moe if he could hit the ball from a conventional stance, which to him would have felt narrow. Moe told him he couldn't hit the ball from there. Craig once wanted to check how far Moe's divot extended past the ball; Moe said it extended fourteen inches, but Craig knew it didn't go that far. It would have been physically impossible to keep the clubface dragging along the ground for that distance. Still, Moe thought he kept the club that low to the ground; it was his way of ensuring he'd swing long and low through the ball. Craig marked the ground with a yellow line ahead of the ball to determine exactly how long Moe's divot did extend. But Moe couldn't hit the ball with the line there. His vision was distorted, and he hit a foot behind the ball. His swing was unique. Nobody else could do what he did, and the best players in the game know this. They talk about Moe reverentially.

Lee Trevino, to CBC's *Fifth Estate:* "I think the guy's a genius when it comes to playing the game of golf. . . . I don't know of any player that I've ever seen that could strike a golf ball like Moe Norman as far as hitting it solid, knowing where it's going, knowing the mechanics of the game and knowing what he wanted to do with the golf club."

Three-time major champion Nick Price: "I've seen Moe hit balls. He's amazing. He's incredibly talented. It's golf in the purest form, as far as I'm concerned."

Ben Hogan watched Moe hit a series of straight shots. Hogan always tried to curve the ball, and he believed that straight shots were accidental, for the same reason that Wally Uihlein, the chairman and CEO of Titleist, has been so interested in the fact that Moe hit the ball with no sidespin. "Just keep hitting those accidents, kid," Hogan told Moe.

Three-time major champion Vijay Singh was asked the

following in a 2004 *USA Today* interview: "Who's the best golfer you've ever seen?" Singh answered, "Moe Norman. I've hit balls with him lots of times. He was incredible. Whatever he said he could do, he could do. If you talk to Lee Trevino and the other greats of the game, they'll tell you how good he was. He could talk it, and he could do it. God gives people little gifts, and Moe had a gift for golf."

Paul Azinger, winner of the 1993 PGA Championship, was a freshman at Brevard Junior College in Florida when Moe turned up at a local driving range. His coach, John Redman, saw Moe and said, "Boys, here comes the best ball-striker that ever lived." "I couldn't believe what I was seeing," Azinger said. "I've hit balls for a couple of hours, it's 100 degrees, and here comes this guy in a long-sleeve turtleneck. I watched him hit drivers at the 250-yard sign, and he never hit one more than ten yards left or right of the marker."

Gary Player won nine major championships. He won the career Grand Slam: the Masters, U.S. Open, Open Championship, and PGA Championship. If the face of a golf club had only one dot on it, and that comprised the hitting area, he said only Moe would have been able to play the game.

Bob Toski was the leading money winner in 1954 on the PGA Tour. He won eleven PGA Tour events and later became one of the game's most noted teachers. He said this of Moe's swing: "It's one of the greatest and strangest actions I've ever seen."

Kel Nagle and Bob Rosburg, each a major champion,

were playing with Moe in the third round at a senior event in Vancouver. Nick Weslock told them before they teed off that they were going to have an interesting round. Moe shot 69, and Nagle said, "It's one of the most amazing exhibitions of ball-striking I've ever seen. If he hadn't let the twelfth green bug him, when his approach sucked back into the rough, I think he'd have shot 63 or 64, because he was four-under through eleven holes. But he kept repeating what happened." He was referring to what Moe considered a bad break on the twelfth green, which led him to make mistakes on the remaining holes and miss birdie opportunities.

•

AFTER THE 2011 MASTERS, I TRAVELED to Pinehurst No. 2, where I'd been invited along with a couple of colleagues to play with Ben Crenshaw, and the conversation turned to Moe. Crenshaw told me of the time he saw Moe do a clinic at the National Golf Club of Canada in Woodbridge, Ontario. Crenshaw was playing a skins game there with Nick Price, Nick Faldo and Fred Couples. Moe hit balls for the golfers and spectators. Crenshaw remembered the precision with which Moe hit every shot. Crenshaw himself was a stylist, a golfer who played with flair and imagination. He liked the fact that Moe was himself and maintained his way of swinging until the end. I could hear in his voice a tone that suggested more golfers would be better off if they found their own way of playing the game. It's difficult to change one's swing, as challenging, and unlikely, as changing one's signature. Crenshaw had tried to alter his swing when he thought it wasn't right; in particular, he'd tried to shorten his backswing. But that was like speaking a different language. He couldn't do it and stopped trying to do it.

Harry White, a sixty-six-year-old Vancouver golf pro who has worked extensively with junior golfers, was sixteen when he first encountered Moe. This was at the Marine Drive Golf Club, where White frequently caddied for the head professional and three-time PGA Tour winner Stan Leonard. Leonard tied for fourth in the 1958 and 1959 Masters and won eight Canadian PGA Championships. His fellow players considered him one of the finest ball-strikers in the game. Leonard admired Moe and often spoke about him with the teenager who was caddying for him. White made sure he watched Moe when he played at Marine Drive. White was mesmerized because he'd never seen anybody hit every shot where he wanted it to go while taking no time over the ball. These observations, and those that tour pros have been making for years about Moe, again raise the question of why he didn't succeed at the game's highest levels.

White pinpointed one possible reason. "He was entertaining," he told me one evening during the week of the 2011 RBC Canadian Open, being held at the Shaughnessy Golf and Country Club. "Moe hit the ball differently than anybody I'd seen. I couldn't stop watching him. I was too shy to talk to him, and he thought people were laughing at him. He would bark at people." They didn't know how to react to him, and he was skeptical, and even frightened, of their approach to him.

Trevino, perhaps more than any other of golf's elite players, seems to understand Moe. He came out of a poor background in Texas and, like Moe, was not to the country club born. He didn't know his father, and he learned the game as a caddy. Trevino's style is unconventional, but his reputation as one of the game's most accurate golfers — ever — endures. He won two U.S. Opens, two Open Championships, and two PGA Championships, all the while standing to the ball with his feet pointed well left of his target and swinging the club in a manner very different from that of most tour pros. Trevino plays very quickly, like Moe did.

Whenever I speak with Trevino, we talk about Moe. He feels compassion toward him. As he told the *Fifth Estate*, he thinks that "Moe just didn't want to deal with the media and to deal with the public. Moe wanted to play golf, and he wanted to win tournaments, . . . [but] he's a very shy person — that's the one thing you have to remember about Moe Norman. . . . He likes to be around his friends, and when you play golf and you play internationally you're going to meet a lot of people that will try to take advantage of you, number one, and to ask you some questions maybe you don't want to answer, and I don't think Moe ever wanted to be in that situation. I think, if Moe would have wanted to be in that situation, there is no telling what Moe Norman would have won. I think he would have won the U.S. Open; I think he would have won all the tournaments around the world."

His reclusive nature contributed to why Moe played

so quickly. It wasn't only the demands of the sport that made him such a fast player. Again, it's not as if he sat in his room or stood on a practice range and thought about how he could best play golf. He had to play quickly because he was shy. Moe didn't mind people looking at him when he was hitting a golf ball, but he could have done without the walking between shots and from green to tee that golf requires. He felt their eyes on him. He felt them thinking he was different from other golfers, different from them.

I was caddying for the Canadian golfer Jim Nelford in the 1981 Canadian PGA Championship at Westmount when he was grouped with Moe in the third round. Moe's starting time was only a minute away, but Moe hadn't yet arrived on the first tee. The starter was calling for him. But Moe didn't like crowds, especially when they were pressing against a rope to see him. If the golf course was his natural environment, he was most at ease in its open spaces. A tee is a confined space, as is a green. It seems absurd to even refer to either a tee or a green as a "space," because Moe never thought they were, at least not for him. He felt caged, and he felt free only after he hit his tee shot or putted out. Then he could escape to the open areas of the course.

A course was different from a driving range. Moe enjoyed standing on a fixed spot there and hitting balls for hours. He was a showman at a range, and he delivered. He could get into a rhythm by hitting balls one after another. At a course, though, it was only that one shot on the tee, eighteen times over the four hours of a round; he could hit hundreds of balls during that time on a range. On the course, he had to walk onto every tee from the previous green. He had to wait on the tee if he wasn't up first. That's why he wanted to get to the first tee at Westmount precisely when it was his turn to hit his opening tee shot.

All the spectators and officials were turning their heads in search of Moe. I looked around. Nelford looked around. The starter looked around. No Moe. But then, not thirty seconds before he would have to hit the ball or be penalized, he shuffled onto the first tee, bouncing a ball off the face of his driver. He wasn't concerned. He knew he'd make his starting time. But it would be "his" time. He would get there when he wanted, just in time. (A player who misses a starting time is assessed a two-shot penalty.) "Give me five shots for all I care. I was signing autographs for the kids," Moe told the starter. He walked directly to the spot on the tee that he chose and put his tee into the ground as the starter announced his name. Moe looked quickly down the fairway and then set his club a foot behind the ball and swung. He reached down the fairway with his arms after he made contact with the ball, which flew straight.

Yet something was wrong. Moe had hit a perfect drive, but people were laughing. Nobody seemed to notice the flight of the ball. They focused on his mannerisms. Nelford hit his tee shot after Moe and also found the middle of the fairway. The spectators applauded. He and Moe walked off the tee together. People were still pointing at Moe and laughing.

Spectators have also laughed for years at John Daly, he of the grip-it and rip-it style, the song "All My Exes Wear

Rolexes," his Willy Wonka pants, the wrap-around-his-body swing that sends the ball into the stratosphere, his whacking the ball all over the place in tournaments without apparent concern for the result, his many withdrawals during tournaments, his very public private life that has included alcoholism, his wild gambling stints. Yet he has somehow embraced all the attention his antics have brought him. Of course, Daly won the 1991 PGA Championship and the 1995 Open Championship in St. Andrews. I was at the 1991 PGA in Indianapolis, which was his coming-out party. And it was a party. Hardly anybody knew much about Daly before the tournament, but then the world knew of him after he splayed his personality all over the Crooked Stick Golf Club while winning. I was watching along the last fairway when Daly walked up to the green, a certain winner. The crowd was screaming. Daly thrust up his arms and whipped them round and round. But as the years went on, and his life grew crazier and crazier, I wondered if he really was all that comfortable with what was going on. Clearly, he had serious problems.

I interviewed Daly for The Sports Network when he started shaking during the 1998 Greater Vancouver Open. He was going through detox, and he was in trouble. He had to withdraw from the tournament, and it was my responsibility to interview him if he agreed at that troubling moment. He did agree, and a crowd gathered. Daly spoke of what he'd been going through. The spectators were sympathetic, of course, but only moments before they'd been laughing at him. Still, I never got the sense that their laughter bothered Daly. Or maybe it did. Maybe he was camouflaging his difficulties with being on display at golf tournaments by sinking into his wild off-course life. Who knows?

I do know that it bothered Moe when spectators laughed while following him. It bothered him deeply. "See, that's how it's been all my life," Moe said as the audience laughed at another swing. "Other players hit good shots, and the crowd cheers. I hit a good shot, and they laugh. Nobody claps. It's been that way all my life. I don't know what it is. For years I've been Canada's laughing stock in golf. Eddie Shack in hockey, me in golf."

Shack was a well-known player for the Toronto Maple Leafs. He didn't so much skate down the ice as appear to tramp all over it; he was Charlie Chaplin on skates, his legs and arms and head and shoulders moving in all directions. He appeared to be running, not skating. Shack was the anti-Bobby Orr. Where Orr was graceful, Shack was ungainly. A popular song of the time caught him. It was called "Clear the Track, Here Comes Shack." He splayed himself all over the ice, and spectators laughed. But this didn't bother Shack, as far as I could tell when I saw him play at Maple Leaf Gardens or in televised games.

I also got some insight into him when I was out for an early morning walk in the summer of 2011. I ran into Shack at a Starbucks in north Toronto. He was sitting outside on a patio, holding court. He was wearing a cowboy hat full of autographs, including from former hockey players Johnny Bower, Andy Bathgate, Norm Ullman, Red Kelly and Gordie Howe. In the middle, Moe had printed MOE NORMAN.

Shack was entertaining again. Somebody asked him why he wasn't in the Hockey Hall of Fame. "I'm ignorant, I loved drink too much and I can't read or write. But every time I played, I got twenty goals [a season], and I played offside" (on the opposite wing, that is). Shack was seventy-four, and, although he was obviously annoyed that he wasn't in the Hall of Fame, he was able to laugh at his absence. He'd played hockey his way, and he considered himself a success. His father, he said, had offered some advice to him: "You don't need education to play hockey. All you gotta do is push, slide, shoot the puck, keep two hands on your hockey stick and if you get a chance crank him." Shack was rolling. "I never cared if people laughed at me," he said. "I didn't care if I could read or write. I could probably buy and sell them. I was an ignorant bastard. But my dad always said, 'Never mind behave yourself. Be yourself.'"

Listening to Shack, I thought, well, Moe was always himself, but he was also hurting when in public, or so it seemed to me. Moe splayed himself all over the golf ball, arranging himself over and around it in unusual positions that observers encountering him for the first time had never seen. Clear the course, here comes Moe.

Moe was rattled at Westmount, and it was hard to watch. I wanted to say something to calm him down. He wasn't nervous about playing this national championship, nothing like that, but he was hurting. Moe was in his hometown of Kitchener, and maybe he felt singled out. Just being who he was set him apart. It's as if he had no way of protecting himself. He had all those years of playing competitive golf, with people focusing on him, yet he still seemed to be in distress in a tournament, even lost. I walked alongside him and Nelford down the fairway, and I listened. Moe couldn't wait to get to his ball so that he could return to his comfort zone; he needed to get to the ball and to make his unique, effective swing. He needed the feeling of the ball sticking to the clubface, of his hands reaching for the target.

Moe reached the green of the par-five first hole in three shots. He had a fifteen-foot putt for birdie. Here, on the green, he was that caged animal. He had to do something to dissipate the feeling that everybody was watching him, hovering over him, suffocating him. All those eyeballs were on him, and he sensed they weren't on him for the quality of his golf but for how different he was. Nelford surveyed his putt while Moe talked to me about pages in a book that he was studying. He liked to drive to a quiet spot in the country and listen to tapes about motivation and positive thinking. He told me that people were wasting their minds. Why didn't they study more? Why didn't they learn more?

Then it was his turn to putt. Moe didn't look at the line. He sensed it and set up over the ball. There was that one look at the target, the hole. He made the birdie putt. Why fret over a putt? A golf ball rolling on the green might hit unseen blemishes that could deflect it from its path. Moe could control the flight of the ball through the air. He could feel the wind and take it into account. But a ball on the ground? Anything could happen. Why worry?

We moved along. Moe birdied the third hole, so he was two under par for the round. He walked to the fourth tee.

A lady said, "Go get 'em, Moe." He heard her. He heard everything. "Listen to the people, see what they say," he said to nobody in particular. He shook his head. He felt like a spectacle. He wanted his golf to be the spectacle. In a moment, on the fourth tee, it was.

Moe felt comfortable only when people were looking at his swing, not at him, his clothes or his mannerisms. He needed to swing and then walk to his next shot as quickly as possible. He would start walking after the ball while it was still in the air. The next shot beckoned, the next opportunity for Moe to control the flight of the ball, to settle himself down, to swing the club again. Immediately. The less time he spent over the ball, the less time he'd feel spectators staring at him.

•

I WAS AT THE OCEAN PALM COURSE in Flagler Beach, Florida, with Craig Shankland and Moe one winter, and I wanted to take some photos of Moe hitting balls. He was hitting balls into the sun, so I asked him if he'd turn the other way. Moe turned toward the ninth fairway, where two women were walking down the middle. They were ten yards apart and 200 yards away. Moe was about to hit his four-wood when Shankland suggested he wait until the women were out of the way. Moe said, "Watch, they'll never know." He hit the ball right between them. They never did know. Moe held out the palm of his hand and added, "The ball will fit on there. The ball will fit on there. I'm the only one who can make it fit, the only one."

"Nobody will ever be like him," Shankland wrote five days after Moe died. He'd started to put together his thoughts about his friend. "Watching him hit balls was riveting. You could not believe how good it was, time after time."

But could anyone really copy Moe's swing? Shankland used to ask Moe if a golfer should emulate him. "He would laugh. 'How can anyone copy my swing, the guys in the white coats would come and take you away. You can't be me. How can you be me? Everyone is copying everyone else, everyone is copying.' Moe would laugh mockingly. 'Be yourself, be yourself,' he would yell. 'Don't try to be me. You can't be me.'"

•

ON ONE OCCASION, I TRIED to imitate Moe during an outing at the Adios Golf Club in Coconut Creek, near Fort Lauderdale. Tom Stewart, the head professional then, had invited me to introduce Moe at a clinic for the members and then to play with Moe and Mike Smith, a player on the Champions Tour. I've tried to swing like far too many players in the course of my golfing life, which has only helped my handicap go from a low of two to nine as I write. I suffer from swing confusion. I've enjoyed writing instruction books with George Knudson, Nick Price and David Leadbetter, and I've written hundreds of articles about the swing. I've been confused, although from time to time I thought that I'd come across something that would work for a long time. That's been an illusion or a delusion. Meanwhile, a room downstairs in my house is full of swing gizmos. They have also found a home in our garage. My wife, Nell, calls the swing gizmo room the pro shop. I've joked that I want my epitaph to read, "Finally, no more swing thoughts." I appear to be deep in thought in a photo of myself at eighteen months old. Nell has written across the top, "Swing thoughts." She's probably right.

I mention this only to suggest that I was in character when I tried to swing like Moe, whether while practicing or during rounds. I was possessed. Moe hit the ball surpassingly well, and to me everything he did made sense. Of course I'd try to swing like him. Never mind that he'd hit 800 balls a day to groove his swing.

In trying to swing like Moe, I had to overcome my inhibitions about how I looked while imitating him. Now I was the one standing far from the ball, arms stretched to the limit, clubhead a foot behind the ball. I had to allow instinct to take over when I'd allowed years of instruction to squelch it. I had to glance briefly at my target and swing. I had to *play* golf and not *think* golf. I had to react, not create.

Holding the club in my palms, I hit balls on the range before we played that day at Adios. I did this again when I tried to emulate Moe during a game at the Medalist Golf Club in Hobe Sound, Florida. Each time I thought I needed to declare to my playing companions that I was trying to emulate Moe, as if it weren't apparent. I think it was my way of saying, "Look, I'm going to be doing something very different here, even weird. Don't mind me, but I need to try this. It makes so much sense to me." I was engaged in an experiment, and the course was my laboratory. At the same time, I was probably setting myself up for failure, or maybe I feared looking so different. Moe looked different every time he hit a golf shot. I'd learned over the years that it wasn't easy for Moe to stick out as he did. But he'd never veered from his way. Why did I care about how I looked over the ball?

It was easier to relax, though, once I'd announced my intention. Soon, during each round, I was hitting the ball with control. Although my handicap had reached that low of two, and I'd played the Ontario and British Amateurs, I'd always thought my swing depended too much on timing. It was "handsy." I played well when my timing was on but felt like a fifteen-handicapper when it wasn't. I was an insecure golfer, never sure how I'd play on any given day. Swinging like Moe, or at least trying to, I thought my backswing was short and tight. I didn't feel my hands and arms flailing in space. I thought I was swinging above the platform of my widely separated feet. The best feeling was through the ball. The sensation was of my clubface sticking to the ball and my arms extending far down the line, toward the target. It was as if I were shaking hands with the flagstick, to use one of Moe's terms.

It became clear to me that I was trying on an imagined golf self while emulating Moe. The enclosed yet large space of a golf course invited me to try to be another golfer or maybe the golfer I really, truly, had inside me. (Yeah, sure.) But we do this all the time in golf, and it feels safe. Golf, after all, is only a game, no matter how seriously we take it.

Golf instruction offers the promise that a golfer

can change. It's self-help and self-improvement, mediated through the swing. I swing, therefore I become . . . somebody else, a new golfer, a renewed golfer. Maybe my imagined golf self could become my real golf self, and I could exert control over the ball. I felt better about myself after a game of golf in which I'd controlled the flight of the ball, and my self-image suffered when my swing got away from me. This was baffling. I knew, intellectually, that I was not my golf swing, that my golf swing was not me. Yet I still thought that life was better, and that I was better, when I controlled the golf ball. I wasn't proud of that feeling. But it was authentic.

The way I played the par-five seventh hole at the Medalist has stayed with me. The ground was fast and firm, which meant a drive hit even slightly awry with too much curve could run through the fairway and into the pine straw and trees. A small pot bunker eats into the fairway some thirty yards short of the green, while another deep pot bunker protects the right front of the green. The smallish green itself runs away hard on the right side. A ball hit to that side can run and run and stop in the trees.

My arms felt connected to my chest as I took the club back on my drive. I felt no clubhead flutter. I swung through the ball and had that sensation of the ball sticking to the clubface. The club felt long, almost as if it were attached to my arms. The ball came off the face right out of the middle. I could hardly even feel the hit because, I suppose, I managed to truly swing through the ball and not at it. The ball hardly curved at all and rolled to a stop well down the fairway. I intentionally hit a low, hooking three-wood for my second shot so that I could have a favorable angle to a back-right hole location. The ball reacted exactly as I'd intended. My thirty-yard pitch shot was crisp, took one hop and spun out a couple of feet from the hole. I made the short birdie putt. Could golf be this easy? Was this the command Moe felt on every shot? If so, it wasn't surprising that hitting golf shots gave him such satisfaction and made him so happy.

As for me, the command I felt at Adios and the Medalist, especially on its seventh hole, evaporated during each round, never to return. I lost the feel in each round when I was faced with a shot over water. The eighth hole at the Medalist is a long par-three. The day I played it the carry to the green was about 190 yards. I felt good over the ball but didn't trust my downswing and flailed at the ball with my arms. My first tee shot went left, away from the water and into the woods. I wanted to see if I could quickly recapture the feel of the swing I was trying to make but twisted my hands at impact on my second tee shot. That one also went into the woods. The same thing happened on the third shot. Just like that, I'd left the realm of instinctive golf and moved into that of thinking or forced golf. I felt a fear of hitting the ball into the water and couldn't lose the feeling. I'd let go of my swing thoughts and expressed my version of Moe's swing. But I was no longer able to let go. I'd had the long line through the ball that was central to Moe's swing. But then, out of fear of the water, I'd tried to throw my upper body, arms and hands at the ball. The long line was gone. Moe was gone. I'd returned.

•

COULD THERE BE A MORE APPROPRIATE name for a golf tournament to start the season than Eager Beaver? That was
what a popular tournament for amateurs at the Uplands
Golf Club was called. It was held at that course in Thornhill,
Ontario, just north of Toronto, every May, and I played it
regularly from the mid-1960s for fifteen years or so. The
top amateurs in the province usually played it, and a feeling of excitement prevailed. I was hardly a top amateur, but
my handicap was low enough for me to get in. I was also a
member at Uplands, which the renowned Canadian archi-
tect Stanley Thompson had designed in the 1920s. Uplands
defined casual golf. Members weren't country-clubbers, so
I felt comfortable there. It was the first course I joined in
Toronto, and I'm sure I'd still be a member there if the
course were still intact. The owners of the land decided to
turn the property into high-end housing in the late 1980s,
and that was it for Uplands as an eighteen-hole course.
Nine holes are still in play, including the par-three, 225-
yard eighth hole, which was the seventeenth hole when the
course was eighteen holes. The hole doesn't have a bunker
and plays from an elevated tee to an elevated green, with
forest all around. The hole should be declared a historic site,
if there were such a designation for classic works.

Many of us referred to Uplands by a rather unpleasant
name, the Pit. I'm not sure why, except that we meant to
give it a name that would reflect how far removed it was
from swanky, white-collar country clubs in Toronto. We also

called it the Home of Golf because we felt at home there. Moe also felt at home at Uplands. He'd won the Beaver, as we called the tournament, when he was an amateur. Uplands was on his golf route. He dropped by regularly because he felt accepted there. Nobody cared what he wore or how he talked or how many Cokes he drank. We were golf geeks before anybody used the word *geek*. Moe fit right in, and he thought the par-seventy course was a solid test of shotmaking. The course played up and down and across rolling terrain. The greens were small, the penalties for missing a shot were often severe and even top-notch players had trouble matching par. It didn't matter that the course was less than 6,000 yards. We did manage to find a few extra yards eventually and got the length just over 6,000 yards. I have a scorecard that had Uplands at 6,001 yards. This included the ninety-five-yard thirteenth hole, which we called Dogmeat. We played for quarters or, when some of us felt flush, a buck for Dogmeat — closest to the hole on the four par-threes, that is. The thirteenth was a tricky little hole. It played over a no-man's-land valley to a tiny green. One player made double figures there when he was leading the club championship in the last round.

Moe showed up at every Eager Beaver. He'd cruise up in his Cadillac, find a quiet place to park, in a corner away from other cars if possible, and amble down to the first tee before play began. The tournament organizers invited Moe to put on a clinic every year. That was the right way to start the season, with Moe showing us how to control the flight of the ball.

The first hole at Uplands is a 330-yard par-four. The tee is slightly elevated. A stream crosses the fairway about 220 yards out, while the fairway starts falling toward the water at 190 yards. The first tee shot of the day is obviously a layup. But Moe would perform his magic long before he'd choose a club to play a shot to the top of the slope.

"Which floor do you want, which floor?" Moe asked and then answered his own question. "Okay, first floor," and he would chip a shot some thirty or forty yards and maybe fifteen feet off the ground. "Second floor now, second floor," and Moe would hit a slightly higher shot. He was laughing, playing with the golf ball and changing the height with every shot. He warmed up, and then he was ready for the main part of the show.

A hydro wire stretched out across the first fairway, seventy-five yards down. A local rule at Uplands allowed players to replay their tee shots when they hit the wire. This rarely happened, but when it did occur it was accidental. But Moe told us he would intentionally hit the wire, about fifty feet above the ground. "Watch, watch," Moe said as he tilted his upper body back so that he could more easily hit the ball high. He couldn't use a wedge because the height he needed meant he wouldn't be able to hit the ball the required seventy-five yards. Instead, he went down to an eight- or nine-iron, gripped down on the shaft and then swung. Year after year, he hit that hydro wire two or three times out of ten. I wouldn't believe this story if somebody told it to me. But I saw Moe do it. He hit that pesky hydro wire, and then he laughed and laughed. He took such satisfaction in hitting the wire. He was a man playing with a golf ball.

That's how Moe approached golf. He couldn't abide golf as work. Play, yes. His swing enabled him to play golf rather than think golf. He played with the golf ball. He toyed with the golf ball. That's all he ever wanted to do.

The golf course was the only place I felt comfortable.
Away from the course I wasn't in my world. But on the
course I was in Moe Norman's world. — Moe, 1983

ENCOUNTERS

LOOKING BACK, I REALIZE I thought the best way to try to know Moe would be to spend as much time as I could with him and not only at tournaments. Sure, following him while he competed was important. But I also wanted to see how he moved through his life. How did he spend his time? This was the old "fly on the wall" idea. I remembered an approach to studying a person that came right out of my introductory psychology classes. It was called "naturalistic observation." Get out there with the person. Watch him. Travel with him. I wanted to hang around, one of my favorite ways of spending time. I took the opportunity to do that with Moe whenever it came up. It didn't hurt that I was writing professionally by the time I decided to observe

Moe again; I felt that much more compelled to try to see what he was all about so I could write about him. The questions I had about him when I first met him remained, as did my fascination with him.

I started my golf column in the *Globe and Mail* in 1980, the same year that a Toronto-based company began *Score Magazine*, now *ScoreGolf*. The *Globe and Mail* was Canada's national paper, and *Score Magazine* was Canada's national golf magazine. I'd read the *Globe and Mail* since I was a kid and golf magazines from the time I started to play golf. I still have many copies of the original *Golf Digest*, when it really was digest size. I have copies of the first few issues of *Sports Illustrated* and the issues in which Ben Hogan, with the consummate help of writer Herbert Warren Wind, published a series of instructional articles. They turned into *Five Lessons: The Modern Fundamentals of Golf*. It's the best-selling golf book of all time. Somebody once said that golf translates oddly well into words. Golf, to me, was about so much. Every player had a story. I'd been trying to grasp Moe's story since I met Moe when I was a teenager. I was thirty-two in 1980 when I started writing for the *Globe and Mail* and editing *Score Magazine* and was still trying to understand him. But, more than anything, I just liked to watch him and be around him. That's what I started to do whenever I could.

CALGARY, 1983

Does anybody really know where a career begins? We look at turning points, roads taken and roads not taken, places where key events happened. Moe figures one place more than any other set him on his way, the Calgary Golf and Country Club. "Golf-wise, Calgary is like a home," Moe told me when we cruised around the city. "The Calgary Country Club made me known as an amateur, and Willow Park [another Calgary course] made me known as a pro. Nice places, what I call nice. Class, especially Willow. The first time I saw it I liked it. It made me feel at home, away from home." He won the 1955 Canadian Amateur at the Calgary Country Club and the 1966 Canadian PGA Championship at the Willow Park Club. He won his three Alberta Opens in Calgary.

Moe is driving his big Cadillac around Calgary today, early in the week of a Senior PGA Tour event at the Earl Grey Golf Club. Moe never drives fast. It's always the inside lane for him, not the passing lane. "Why rush, what's the hurry, what's the hurry?" He takes me to a workman's shed at Willow Park. We walk in. "The first place I come to in Calgary is here. Put your pant leg up against the wall. There's no dirt. Nice, what I call nice."

We pull into the club where he won the 1955 Canadian Amateur, his first national championship. Moe points to the hole where he won the championship at twenty-five years old in a sudden-death playoff over local favorite Lyle Crawford. They had played the full thirty-six holes of their final match and were tied. Moe had lost the Ontario Amateur earlier in the summer at Westmount in Kitchener, where he'd been the local favorite. Jerry Magee, a top-notch amateur who would go on to be the head professional at St.

George's Golf and Country Club in Toronto, had beat him on the first extra hole. "This is where I won the Canadian Amateur," Moe says as we walk toward the hole. "Thirty-ninth hole, I hit a drive and a six-iron, par-four, 426 yards, and I birdied it. I played it the other day and birdied it again." Time collapses for Moe, nearly thirty years later. He shakes his head. He tosses his head.

Now he's back at Westmount that summer of 1955, where he lost to Magee. The loss seemed to convince people that he was going nowhere. "Everybody said, 'Aw, he'll never be any good. He doesn't take any time. He just gets up and hits it.' Two weeks later I come out here, and I win the Canadian Amateur."

There's the Bow River, flowing through the course. Moe walks to the bank. "I wasn't at the presentation. I was hiding over here. As soon as I holed out, I went and hid."

•

INTROVERT. TRY THE WORD OUT for a moment. Does it apply to Moe? Most introverts don't want to be in a crowd, to work a crowd. They prefer not to speak to a crowd. No microphones for them. But do they also feel stupid? Moe felt stupid. Think about the hurt a person who calls himself stupid must feel. Think about that person at a golf tournament, doing one thing exceptionally well. That's all the person wants to do. Why does somebody who hits a golf ball beautifully have to speak anyway? Why should public speaking be part of the job description for a tournament golfer? Professional golf isn't entertainment, even if it can be entertaining to watch.

And why did people laugh when Moe hit that damn ball exactly where they wanted him to hit it, exactly where he aimed it? They didn't laugh when Ben Hogan or Jack Nicklaus did that. They didn't laugh at Tiger Woods when he was pulling off shots that players found, as Ernie Els once said, "unbelievable." They didn't laugh when Rory McIlroy, only twenty-two, crushed the field in the 2011 U.S. Open to win by eight shots. "Let's go, Rory, let's go, Rory," they cheered as he walked the fairways of the Congressional Country Club's Blue course outside Washington, DC. Everybody remarked on his elegant swing. He hit the ball, with elegance, where he was looking. Moe hit the ball, with a swing deemed awkward, where he was looking.

Golfers who succeed at the highest levels don't look like Moe, do they? They look, well, normal. They dress the way golfers are supposed to dress. Their toes aren't sticking out of their shoes. They're not wearing turtlenecks in ninety-degree heat. They wait until the announcer finishes introducing them on the first tee before they hit their shots. Moe was just being himself, wasn't he? Was he hurting anybody? He was playing golf the only way he knew, quickly, eyes on the target, club swinging toward it.

•

THIS IS 1983, MANY YEARS AFTER MOE HID by the Bow River after winning the Canadian Amateur. The golf world has been used to Moe for decades. He's won almost everything in Canada, starting with that 1955 Canadian Amateur.

He won it the next year as well. Now he's playing with the big boys on the Senior PGA Tour. Why, right now he's participating in a clinic at Earl Grey, in advance of the tournament, and the 1968 Masters champion, Bob Goalby, is asking Moe to play a shot. "Moe, let's see you hit a little six-iron ankle high."

Moe hears the command, and his body reacts. You'd think somebody threw him a baseball and he's reacted. Hands out, ball caught. But, no, the golf ball is on the ground. Moe has to start his swing. There's nothing to react to but Goalby's order.

Not a word, just the steel of the clubshaft moving back along the ground and then rising slightly. Arms connected to Moe's chest. Arms and shoulders a V. Feet planted so solidly on the ground you'd think he's in ankle irons. Now back to the ball, clubface seeming to stick to the ball as it pours through it, the ball taking off. Ankle high. Command fulfilled.

Applause, you'd think. You'd be wrong.

"Everybody laughed like hell," Moe said to me later. He hit the ball like a machine, but spectators still couldn't move beyond his mannerisms to appreciate the artistry. "I hit it right down along the ground, and everybody's laughing like hell." He hit that ankle shot the way Goalby wanted him to, and all he got was laughter. I heard appreciation in the laughter, though. The spectators were laughing because it was absurd that a golfer could instantaneously react, on command, to hit such a shot. People do laugh sometimes when somebody performs in a way far beyond what they could do or what they expect. Yet Moe heard scorn.

●

Arnold Palmer and Don January are also at this Senior PGA Tour event. They are winners of major championships. Arnie is the king, as everybody calls him, although he tells me years later that he's never liked the word. Moe says he used to feel he belonged in the shithouse, not the clubhouse. Even today he doesn't like going into clubhouses. A few hours ago he took his golf shoes out of the trunk of his Cadillac and put them on there. He's the quintessential trunk-slammer.

Moe's a golfer, that's all. We want to make him something else, but he's exclusively a golfer. And when a person swings like Moe, isn't that enough? Who wouldn't want to follow him wherever he's playing? You like jazz, you try to catch John Coltrane or Wynton Marsalis. You like film, you watch Marlon Brando, Katharine Hepburn, George Clooney, Al Pacino, Helen Mirren, Jack Nicholson.

Marsalis once said this:

> We're all given the gift of creativity. It comes out in all kinds of ways — the way we talk or dress or cook or whistle. I remember when I was a kid my friends and I used to see who could cut grass in the most creative way. But many times young people are put down for having a gift or skill that doesn't fit with somebody else's idea of what he or she should do with their lives. Jazz is the opposite of that. It tells you, "That's you! Take pride in this

thing. Express yourself. Your sound is unique. Work on it. Understand it." Often it teaches you to celebrate yourself.

Golf is also an art, like music or theater or even dance. Yes, dance. Percy Boomer wrote a book called *On Learning Golf*. He included a chapter called "As a Dancer Sees It." The dancer wasn't a golfer, but she saw how the golfer swinging a club was dancing in place with the club swishing and moving in space as the golfer danced and celebrated himself. The golfer makes the dance happen.

Or, in Moe's case, *lets* it happen. "*Let*, that's the biggest word in golf," Moe says. I've heard his mantra before. It's part of his golf rap. I think he's offering a lesson without meaning to. He's telling me not to get in my own way, to let "me" out. He's let himself out. Figured he was in a cage back home and in school. Didn't fit. He found refuge on the golf course. It was his sanctuary, except that Moe had trouble with the folks who watched and they with him.

•

AFTER THE PGA EVENT IS OVER, we're back in his Cadillac meandering along Calgary roads. His mind rolls back to 1958, twenty-five years earlier. He's just won the Ontario Open at the Cataraqui Golf and Country Club in Kingston, during his first year as a professional. It's three years after Moe hid on the banks of the Bow River during the prize ceremony after winning the Canadian Amateur. He's been winning big Canadian tournaments. People want to hear him speak. Why won't they leave me alone? Why isn't it enough that I just play golf? Can't they see that's all I want to do? I like to hit balls, and I like to make that ball go where I want it to go, and, if that wins the tournament, beautiful. Beautiful. But I'm not thinking about that. I'm just trying to play. Leave me alone.

Jack Bailey owns the Pine Valley Golf Club in the northwest Toronto suburb of Woodbridge. Bailey has taken an interest in Moe. "He liked me because I was so different," Moe says, remembering that 1958 Ontario Open. "He loves me. For a millionaire, he put me under his wings like I was one of his sons."

The millionaire tells Moe at Cataraqui to grab the mike, that's all, just grab the mike. Hold it as if it's just another club. Nothing to fear. But Moe's pal Nick Weslock always said that a phone was like a cobra in Moe's hands. Moe has never owned a phone. He doesn't take calls wherever he happens to be living. If you want to reach Moe, maybe you can get a message to him, and maybe he'll meet you at a course. But talk on the phone? Not likely. A mike is a lot like a phone.

"Just take that mike and say thanks, just say the word *thanks*," Bailey encourages Moe. "That'll get you started. Get the feeling of holding the mike and saying thanks. If you can say more, go ahead."

Moe takes the mike at Cataraqui and says thanks. It's a start.

Bailey's advice helps. Moe wins the 1963 Ontario Open, and Bailey tells him again to take the mike and say thanks. "I did, just a little more," Moe tells me as we drive around

Calgary. He wins a tournament at Pine Valley the next year. "I made a little longer speech. And here I am today."

Here he is today, in Calgary. Moe would be okay with saying a few words or more than a few words. He has a rap. He's been studying the game, and he says he's been studying the mind, and he's rolling now as we roll along the roads in his Caddy. He's fifty-three years old, and he knows his best tournament days are behind him, but golf is a game for a lifetime, as they all say, and he believes he has something to say to young people in particular. He loves to be around young people.

A couple of years earlier Moe was flying to Vancouver for a tournament. He was waiting in the Toronto airport for his flight, half an hour until boarding. He noticed a kid nearby. Moe pulled out a couple of golf balls from his pocket. He always carried a couple of golf balls. *Always.* They were his talismen, his connection to who he was, what he did.

"I'm sitting on the floor with my legs apart, and I'm rolling a ball at a kid. I don't even know who she is. I'm rolling one at her, she's rolling one at me and the crowd's laughing. A couple of times one ball hit the other. The kid's rolling on the floor, and people are laughing, they're having a great time watching us."

Moe the entertainer. Wordlessly.

Earlier today, at the Senior Tour event, a little girl asked Moe for a photograph. He looked at her and said, "Don't you be crazy like me, don't you be crazy, don't play this crazy game." He enjoyed the moment. "She laughed like hell," he says to me now.

Moe, in his mid-thirties
(COURTESY PGA OF CANADA ARCHIVES)

^ With his close pal Nick Weslock at Heron Point Golf Links in Ancaster, Ontario

(© DON VICKERY PHOTOGRAPHY)

< Extension and a wide stance: two factors that contributed to Moe's precision

(© DON VICKERY PHOTOGRAPHY)

With Lorne at Royal Oak in Titusville, Florida (COURTESY LORNE RUBENSTEIN)

Enjoying the flight of the ball (© DON VICKERY PHOTOGRAPHY) >

This shot must have finished close to the hole

Swinging "through" the course,
not "around" the course

(© DON VICKERY PHOTOGRAPHY)

Before a game with Moe (COURTESY LORNE RUBENSTEIN)

Moe speaks about the importance of the mind at his induction into the Canadian Golf Hall of Fame (© DON VICKERY PHOTOGRAPHY)

Lorne interviewing Gus Maue during Moe's induction
(© DON VICKERY PHOTOGRAPHY)

Moe at the National in Woodbridge, Ontario. Foreground L-R: Fred Couples, Ben Crenshaw, Nick Price, Nick Faldo, Bob Weeks (in black shirt in background), the late Ben Kern — then the National's director of golf — and Jim Deeks (COURTESY GOLF CANADA ARCHIVES)

<   Moe extends down the line toward his target; he called this "shaking hands with the flagstick" (© DON VICKERY PHOTOGRAPHY)

Shaking hands with the flagstick again, as always

(COURTESY PGA OF CANADA ARCHIVES)

While adults often unnerved him, Moe always
liked to be with children (© DON VICKERY PHOTOGRAPHY)

(COURTESY PGA OF CANADA ARCHIVES)

It's a privilege to watch Moe hit golf balls and work his way around a course. It's a revelation to watch him with kids. He's comfortable with them. All the discomfort he feels with adults evaporates when he's with children. He speaks their language. They recognize something in him. Why does Moe feel so at ease with them? Probably because kids are all instinct, and so is he. He knows how to do one thing so well, and he knew how to do it when he was a kid.

"I just love 'em, I just love 'em," Moe says of kids. "I pick 'em up. If I ever won the Canadian Open, I said I'd stay on the steps of the clubhouse, and I'd hope there were 10,000 kids there. I'd say, 'Come on, kids.' I wouldn't sign autographs for grown-up people, but for kids I would sit there all day. I'd sit there all day for kids, because these kids could be something one day. They could be a Moe Norman one day. They still have a future."

A few minutes later we pull over to the side of the road. Moe is listening to positive-thinking tapes. I ask him what they do for him. He says he loves to study, that studying is his new hobby. His trunk is full of books about positive thinking. He memorizes pages that Paul Bertholy, a golf teacher he admires and visits frequently in Pinehurst, has written. The words start slowly, and then they're a waterfall. A wordfall. A torrent.

"People are afraid to win, to become good at the things they do," Moe says. "People can't face reality, they're afraid of it, they're afraid to live. You gotta believe there's no to-morrow and give it the best you have today."

Moe speaks for a moment about Ed Membery, who

contracted polio when he was seven years old and later owned a course an hour north of Toronto called Golf Haven. He employed Moe for a few years, gave him a place to play and practice, made him feel at home.

"Overnight he got polio," Moe says. "You gotta believe there's no tomorrow."

Moe is quiet for a second. He's sad. Now he's off again.

"Vanity is the luxury of fools. A missed golf shot will never hurt my golf swing, only my vanity. Don't be afraid to make a mistake. Now I'm not. I used to be afraid to make a mistake. No more. Boy, has it ever changed my life. Now I make less mistakes because I'm not afraid to make them. People make mistakes every day."

Moe starts the engine, and we drive some more. Calgary has changed. "This used to be a two-lane road. Now it's four, and they have eight- and ten- and twelve-lane roads now. Isn't that something?"

I don't want to intrude upon his line of thinking. I don't even know if he's thinking, and instead I just take in the stream-of-consciousness monologue. He's just going. He's moving. I can't guess at the destination.

"The practice of perfection makes perfect, not just practice. There's no such thing as perfect. I shot 59 once at Rockway. I made a bogey, so it wasn't perfect."

Here's the card, dated July 16, 1957, from that 59. Moe was playing with Gary Cowan (67), Lloyd Niziol (75) and Bob Patterson (80). The card: par, par, birdie, par, par, par. One-under after six holes. Eagle, birdie, birdie. Five-under (30) after nine holes. Bogey, birdie, par, par. Five-under after thirteen holes. Birdie, eagle, birdie, birdie. Ten-under after seventeen holes. Birdie on eighteen. Eleven-under after eighteen. In the end, 59.

"I made a bogey, so it wasn't perfect."

ONTARIO SENIOR PGA CHAMPIONSHIP, BAYVIEW GOLF AND COUNTRY CLUB, TORONTO, AUGUST 28–29, 1986

An Ontario PGA Official is at the first tee handing out pin sheets to competitors, but Moe doesn't bother picking one up. He tells the official that the greens are so small he doesn't need them. He's wearing red-and-green plaid slacks, a green turtleneck, although it's a hot day, and brown shoes. He wears turtlenecks in the heat because he burns easily. Moe picks up a Diet Coke and points to his slacks. "Look at these, look. They're thirty-eights, but I need thirty-six or thirty-seven. I don't have the money to buy pants. You need forty or fifty dollars to get anything good." He says he has $800 left. "Two more months, that's it. Then it will be time to pack it in."

Moe bounces a ball on the face of his Power-Bilt driver, sticks a tee into the ground and steps up to the ball. He swings. Perfectly. As always, Moe draws a few laughs.

"You didn't get all of that one, did you?" somebody asks.

Moe replies, "Cruising for a bruising already, are you? I'm six inches off line, and you're giving me a lesson."

A fellow on the practice putting green adjacent to the first tee asks, "Did you hit another fairway, Moe?"

Moe can't let the comments go as he walks down the first fairway. "Six inches off line, and he gives me hell, I hit the best drive of my life, and he gives me hell." But then

Moe laughs. He's joking around. It's not always easy to discern whether he is truly hurt or just joking around. He seems to be developing a tougher hide.

Moe continues down the fairway, bouncing a ball off the clubface — that second ball he carries in his pocket. He lays up his second shot on the par-five, but the ball trickles into the left rough. Moe is surprised. "I thought I hit a perfect second." He then hits his third shot twenty-five feet from the hole. On the green now, Moe sets up. He hasn't lined up his putt from behind, the sides or the other side of the hole. He takes two practice strokes and rolls his long birdie putt into the hole, dead center. He's started with a birdie and congratulates himself. "Good four there, four on this hole, are you kidding, in this cold weather?"

Ron Montressor, one of Moe's fellow pros in the group, watches Moe hit another drive down the center line on the next hole. He wonders out loud whether Moe ever gets bored, because every shot is the same. "No, no, I never get tired of the middle," Moe replies. "It's beautiful down there. Lloyd Tucker always told us to keep our toes ahead of our heels and that you can't go wrong that way." That's one way to put it: toes ahead of heels. Walk in a straight line.

Moe is playing quickly, as always. He appears to feel the distance and the line in his bones, trusts his feelings, swings. A pin sheet and a yardage book would only complicate matters for him. "It all registers with me right away," Moe says while walking to the fifth tee. "My first thought is the right one. You'll never see me second-guess myself. I feel it before I hit it."

The fifth hole is a 378-yard par-four that moves right to left, around trees. Moe hits his tee shot over the trees. He felt the shot, he saw the shot and he played the shot. "I feel everything. I like feeling things. I sense it. I feel it. I want that line of compression, the angle of attack."

Moe traces his certainty while playing golf to the way Tucker taught him at Rockway. He wasn't a method teacher. He coached individuals.

"I never changed," Moe says. "Tucker believed in sensation of positions. He was an action man, not a stylist. None of this 'Get your feet here.'"

Moe misses a three-footer on the fifth green after Montressor holes from eight feet. Moe congratulates his friend and, laughing, misses his short putt. Montressor is frustrated. Like many people who observe Moe, he thinks he should take more time with his putts. But that wouldn't be Moe. He's the 747 of golf, after all. And isn't it possible, even likely, that he'd miss the putts he makes by not over-analyzing them? Moe has to play his way.

Harold Bernstein doesn't see it this way, at least when Moe misses short putts. Bernstein, a local pro and a pal of Moe's, is in the group. "He pisses away so many strokes," Bernstein says. "I keep telling him his head is moving."

Moe won't have any of it. There's something of the way Ben Hogan and George Knudson felt about putting in the way Moe thinks. They cared more about the quality of their full shots than about their putting. To them, the art of the game is in the swing, not on the greens. They could study the swing and come to an understanding of it. But putting? A ten-year-old can often putt better than a tour pro. Figure that out.

"I'm probably the only guy in history who could drive straighter than he putts," Moe says. "Put a tire out there 250 yards or give me a ten-foot putt. I'll hit the tire more often than the hole. I can't feel the putts. A putt isn't nearly like a full shot. It's been that way all my life."

I ask Moe why this is so as he walks along. He tells me that it's because the muscles aren't as involved in the putting stroke as they are in the swing. The swing is physical. The putting stroke isn't. What it is Moe doesn't know. He doesn't understand putting because it's so technical. There's the grain to understand, and the hole is small. The closer he gets to the ultimate target — the hole — the more elusive it becomes. By the time he finishes the front nine, he's made that twenty-five-foot putt on the first hole, missed two putts from three feet and holed an eight-footer. Moe acknowledges he can at least feel the longer putts, if not to the extent he can feel a full swing. He has to move the putter farther; his muscles are slightly involved. Moe points out that there's expectation involved in a short putt; who can miss a three-footer? But golfers throughout the history of the game have had trouble with short putts. The English writer Henry Leach wrote a memorable essay called "The Tragedy of the Short Putt." It's embarrassing to stand over a three-footer and then miss the hole. Golfers sometimes freeze over the ball and have difficulty taking the putter back. The hole is so near, but the possibility of making the putt feels remote. I ask Moe if the expectation of making a short putt introduces a little fear into him.

"Not a little, a lot," Moe tells me.

He walks on, hitting one perfect tee shot after another, hitting irons to the right spots on the greens, putting inconsistently. I expect Moe to hit fairways and greens, but I feel apprehensive the nearer he gets to the hole. He's a different person on the greens. Moe wanders around as his playing companions putt. He leans on the shaft of his putter, waves the head of his putter at blades of grass. There's a vacancy about him on the greens. No wonder he feels so much more at home on a driving range. Thinking about this, I realize I hardly ever saw him on the putting green at De Haviland. Moe is at home on the range and lost on the greens. Today he seems especially lost on the greens. He misses a few more short putts and shoots 75. Not a good start, but he's okay with the round.

"I did it, nobody else," Moe says. "It's part of the game, that's all. I've never thrown a club. I've never batted a ball off the green. I'm not upset. All you can do is try, all you can do is try."

The weather is milder for the second round, and the wind is down. After the first round, Moe drove into the countryside, parked by the side of a road and read some positive-thinking books and listened to some of the motivational tapes he always has in his car. His game is complete today; he's making the short putts, and he chips in for a birdie on the par-four tenth hole. Moe is dissecting Bayview, in front of a gallery of eight people, including two kids, while hitting sixteen greens in regulation. He shoots

67 and wins the tournament by six shots, picking up $650 for two days of work. It's his forty-ninth victory in tournaments of thirty-six holes or more.

Moe says he'll study some more tonight. "Nothing else to do," he says as he walks to his car. He opens the trunk, takes off his golf shoes and inserts shoe trees. His trunk is loaded with golf balls. He takes off his turtleneck and T-shirt and stands in the parking lot for a moment before he puts on a fresh, yellow, long-sleeve shirt.

A fellow who watched him play comes over and tells Moe, "You can putt with the best of them."

Moe says, "Yeah, but I wish I knew what I was doing." He sees a little girl and tosses a ball to her. "Are you going to hit it like me when you get older?"

The front and back seats in Moe's car are full of tapes and books: *The Wisdom of Your Subconscious* by John K. Williams (which Moe says he's read twenty times), *In Pursuit of Excellence* by Terry Orlick. There's a sheet with tools for stress management that a woman in Florida gave him. Tapes about playing subconscious golf. A pamphlet by golf teacher Bill Skelley on golf dynamics. A small book called *The I Can Discourse*.

"Look, look, look at anything you want," Moe says. "Relaxation, mental imagery, dimensions of the mind, the management of fear and anxiety. Things people don't know are going on in life. I'm in a world of my own up here. By far."

A reporter tries to interview Moe at his car, but he walks away. The reporter says, "He's a nut. I've never seen a guy carry on like this who isn't a nut." The guy doesn't know Moe and is upset that he's been rebuffed. I wish the reporter would try to understand Moe. At least he doesn't leave as Moe starts to talk to me about being a golf analyst. He uses terms such as "gross energy" and "key energy." The reporter stands nearby, taking it all down. Moe is talking now, freely, but it's hardly an interview.

"I wanna talk about what I wanna talk about, what Moe Norman wants to talk about," Moe says.

The reporter has changed his mind about him. "You're right," he tells me. "He's not crazy. He's just strange. He's different. He's the strangest guy I've ever met."

•

SUMMER ENDS, AND MOE IS running out of money. Gus Maue organizes a benefit for him at Westmount and invites Moe's friends and fellow pros to pay $100 each to attend and help Moe out. The benefit attracts 125 people and raises $12,000 for Moe. He's quiet all night while Maue and others say a few words about him. Moe sits at his table and twirls his fork. He's given a watch but decides he doesn't need it and hands it over to Ed Membery's wife. Moe says he has his golf, and that's enough.

Moe's first swing coach, Lloyd Tucker, is one of the speakers, and his voice breaks while he speaks about Moe, more than forty years after they met at Rockway.

"If you've seen Fred Astaire, you've seen the best dancer," Tucker says. "If you've seen Peggy Fleming, you've seen the best skater. And when you've seen Moe Norman hit a golf ball, you know you've seen the best that ever hit a golf ball."

Moe's friends listen carefully to this high praise. The room is silent except for Tucker. His words touch everybody, and they applaud Moe. They applaud him and applaud him again. Moe stands, looks over the room and waves for some time to his friends.

Later Moe returns to the room in the house he's rented for seventeen summers. He says he's "like a guard almost" in that he does nothing but sleep in the room. "I don't bring in broads. I don't bring in booze. They say I can use the kitchen, but I don't."

What Moe does, mostly, is play golf, hit balls when he's not on the course or study in his car. "I find a quiet spot by the side of the road and study three or four hours in my car. I take a big Diet Coke along and, if I'm hungry, some food. I read the same stuff so I can get it memorized."

Moe lives the same way in Daytona Beach every year from November through April. He's lived in the same bungalow there for twenty years. Moe lives by habit and routine. But he did change something major. He drank twenty Cokes a day for thirty-five years, which must have eroded his teeth and made them resemble fangs, but now he drinks only Diet Coke. He drinks them to keep himself awake during the day. That's his explanation. "Never in my life have I slept during the day. The nights are meant for sleep."

MAPLE DOWNS PRO-AM, AUGUST 1989

Irv Lightstone had run a tournament for years to raise money for Easter Seals. Moe had participated regularly, and this time I was playing with him. He'd turned sixty the previous month, and only the evening before he'd spoken at a dinner after another tournament. Moe was different in some ways than he'd been years ago. He could speak at a function. He still changed clothes in his car and didn't engage much in the social part of the evening. But he was prepared to say a few words at dinner.

"I'm cool now when I grab that microphone," Moe had told me on the course. "Now I grab it like my driver. Before, I could talk out there, on the course, but not inside the clubhouse. I'd put myself on top of a tree on the first tee, but inside the clubhouse I'd feel like I was in a hole."

It was good to hear Moe speak, comfortably and slowly and quietly. He was with friends. He'd come a long way.

CLINIC, NATIONAL GOLF CLUB OF CANADA, AUGUST 25, 1993

Fifty golfers are gathered around Moe on the practice tee at the National on a summer's day. The National is Canada's top-ranked course, and the members are serious golfers. They want to see Moe for themselves, so the club has invited him to hit some balls and talk about what he does. Moe doesn't waste any time with a long preamble, though. The balls are on the turf, and they're like catnip to him. He starts hitting balls almost as soon as he walks onto the range. He's giving a lot of clinics this summer; the Canadian PGA has arranged them for him, and he's paid $800 for each clinic. Moe will do seventy clinics this year. He'll travel outside his usual area of southern Ontario to Winnipeg, Regina, Calgary and Edmonton.

"Let your body memorize your swing," Moe advises as

he fills the sky with golf balls. He doesn't want to have a single swing thought over the ball. See the target, feel the shot, swing. But if he doesn't think over the ball, his mind does contain books of advice. "Two things you got to finish in this game, your backswing and your follow-through," he says, and he does.

PGA TEACHING AND COACHING SUMMIT,
NEW ORLEANS, DECEMBER 1994

Moe, in front of 1,300 teaching pros, talking to them about his swing and his ideas? The very thought that he would stand up in front of such a gathering, which included all the best-known names in teaching and coaching, seems ridiculous. Moe speaks only to his friends or, sometimes, during clinics or dinners after pro-ams in Canada. But he's been invited to address the summit, and he's accepted. He is on the schedule for Friday, December 2, at 10:15 a.m. in the ballroom at the Hyatt Regency New Orleans. I've flown down from Toronto to watch him. I have a hard time believing Moe will show up, because he is so shy and still feels that the golf world at large doesn't accept him or his ideas. Yet it's undeniable: he is on the bill, he has accepted the invitation and, by the buzz building at the summit, everybody is eager to see him and welcome his appearance.

Moe prepared for the summit by spending five hours the previous week with Craig Shankland in Daytona Beach. Moe trusts him. Shankland videotaped Moe on the practice range while they talked. Moe was comfortable. He's always comfortable while hitting balls on a range.

Prone to trying every scrap of instruction I hear, especially from respected teachers, I laugh to myself when the legendary Australian coach Norman Von Nida speaks about grip pressure at the summit. This is shortly before Moe is scheduled to appear. The Von, as he's called, says that a golfer should hold the club with little pressure. "Anybody who chokes the club with the left hand cannot hit the right shot," he says. Moe holds the club in the last three fingers of his left hand in a death grip. Both ideas make sense to me. Not to Moe, mind you, who is convinced his way is the right way, the best way, the only way. He likes to say, "If you can hit it any better, I'll eat your hat."

Here comes Shankland to the stage. Moe isn't with him, and Shankland announces Moe informed him forty-eight hours earlier that he wouldn't attend. People are whispering about his absence. They're disappointed. Shankland says he is certain that anybody who knows Moe understands that appearing in front of more than 1,000 of his peers "would frighten the hell out of him." He adds that, in his opinion, Moe "truly is the world's best ball-striker, a living legend."

The lights in the football-sized ballroom dim as Shankland cues up the tape he made the previous week. It took him twenty hours to edit the material down to thirty minutes for use at the summit.

Moe starts on the range with short shots. "This is what I do so well," he says. "I feel it to the hole." He adds that he thinks he's the only person who can grip a club in the lifeline of his right hand and swing it so that his hands don't twist. "I'm the only person who plays with one straight line," Moe says. "I have the simplest move in golf. I'm never tied up. I'm free as a bird. The ball goes dead straight. I can't hit it crooked if I want to." Moe is in golf heat. He's rapping as he swings. He's cooing. "My left foot takes the hit on every shot. My big toe on my left foot never moves. I'm left-sided in everything."

Lanny Wadkins, winner of the 1977 PGA Championship and twenty-one PGA Tour events, delivers the keynote address at the summit. Butch Harmon, working with a teenage Tiger Woods at the time of the summit, is a speaker. So is Hank Haney, who would later work with Woods; and Rick Smith, then coaching Phil Mickelson. But everybody is talking about Moe as the summit ends. They agree that his appearance at the summit, even by videotape, is the highlight.

CANADIAN GOLF HALL OF FAME INDUCTION, AUGUST 24, 1995
Moe steps outside the modest clubhouse at the Foxwood Golf Club, which Gus Maue owns, and into the heat of a summer evening. He has a putter in his hands, and he puts it behind his shoulders and looks out over the holes. He is quiet. He is happy. He is content. We played a few days ago in Brantford, and he told me had just bought a "big new Cadillac Fleetwood." Moe pronounced it "gorgeous." He also said during our round that nobody teaches the middle of the golf swing. "It's not taught at all, they only teach the start and the finish, to grab the end of the club and swing the end. As I go back, my left knee is starting toward the target. For me and Hogan, the left knee is setting the angle of the downswing." Moe comes out with information like

this during a round. He also cleaned the grooves of his irons as we walked along the course, and told me that Cary Middlecoff, the 1955 Masters champion, advised him to do this the following year at the Masters. "He said you should always have a clean clubface and a clean ball. That way you don't put any more hazards into the game."

Moe is being inducted into the Canadian Golf Hall of Fame, and it's about time. Gus and his family own the twenty-seven-hole public course. "He feels comfortable here," Maue says as forty friends and family celebrate Moe's induction at Foxwood.

The Canadian Golf Hall of Fame was founded in 1971, but Moe wasn't in the inaugural class of six inductees; nor was he among the inductees over the next twenty-three years. It wasn't until February 1995 that the Royal Canadian Golf Association's Hall of Fame committee announced that he'd been selected for induction, with the ceremony to occur later that year.

Moe should have been inducted much earlier given his accomplishments. He'd won at the national level often. His national championships alone should have been enough to gain him admission. Did the fact that he was so "outside" the Canadian golf establishment have anything to do with the glaring omission? Perhaps Moe had embarrassed the powers-that-be when he walked away from Augusta in the third round of the 1956 Masters. Or maybe he'd made things worse by getting kicked off the Canadian team for the Americas Cup the following year.

I wondered. It didn't make sense that Moe hadn't been

inducted into the Hall of Fame for so many years. It was impossible not to think that he had been wronged.

In the fall of 1993, the RCGA announced that amateur Bob Wylie and professional Cathy Sherk would be inducted into the Hall of Fame. Their inductions eventually took place in the spring of 1995 as part of the RCGA's centennial year celebrations. Wylie had won six of the last nine Canadian Senior Amateur Championships, while Sherk had won two Canadian Ladies Championships and the 1978 U.S. Women's Amateur Championship. Each was worthy of induction. But so was Moe, again passed up. I asked why and was told that nobody had nominated him until his close pal Nick Weslock did so, in December 1992. It wasn't widely known that anybody could offer a candidate. Still, it was strange that nobody within the higher echelons of Canadian golf had thought of nominating Moe all those years.

His nomination came in the form of Weslock's letter to the Royal Canadian Golf Association. Ralph Costello, chairman of the Canadian Golf Hall of Fame's selection committee, wrote to Weslock in June 1993 to tell him that the letter had been accepted as a nomination. He wrote in the letter, "All committee members, of course, are familiar with Moe's career, and details of his record will be compiled for assessment." He added, "While there have been some comments and some speculation about why Moe is not in the Golf Hall of Fame, the fact is he had not been nominated."

Weslock's letter wasn't the only document sent to Costello in support of Moe. Ron Rayner, the head professional at the Summit Golf and Country Club in Richmond Hill, Ontario, and Joe Robert, an RCGA honorary governor, wrote to him on April 22, 1993, to nominate Moe. They included his tournament record and wrote that "Moe is well known to most of the golfing world, and we feel that his record more than justifies him for acceptance into the Hall of Fame."

Costello told me in late October 1993, following the announcement of Wylie's and Sherk's impending inductions, that Weslock's nomination of Moe hadn't yet been considered because documentation about him hadn't been gathered. Ten months had passed since Weslock's original letter and six months had passed since Rayner and Robert had written to Costello.

I asked around further. A Canadian golf insider who would later be inducted into the Hall of Fame but who didn't want to be identified thought that Moe didn't belong. "Why is his name popping up all of a sudden?" he asked me. "Yes, he's a great striker of the ball, but what did he accomplish nationally and internationally?" He believed the fact that Moe was now up for consideration was "really sentimental" and added, "There is more to the game than striking the ball. That's maybe twenty percent of it." The fellow went on: "I don't think the RCGA had a grudge against Moe. I'm a little torn since he's a popular figure. But you have to look objectively and ask what he did internationally. This is a golf hall of fame. I think it should be about accomplishments. A golfer could be known around the world, but he could be known as a buffoon."

Many people viewed Moe exactly that way.

Weslock said, simply, "I go by the record. Moe's is out-standing, as far as I'm concerned."

Costello agreed. "Moe has been unique in Canadian golf. One of his contributions to golf in Canada is as a superb striker of the ball. But it's more than that. He has won two Amateurs, something of significance. His tournament record is not the greatest nationally and internationally, but he has been around a long time and is worthy of consideration and will be given that consideration."

A nomination is active for five years. In the spring of 1994, Paul Sherratt, head professional at the Rideau View Club in Manotick, near Ottawa, and Canadian PGA representative to the Hall of Fame committee, made a strong presentation in support of Moe's induction. Keith Rever, then chairman of the selection committee, announced in a release on February 20, 1995, that Moe would be inducted into the Canadian Golf Hall of Fame that year. Jack Nicklaus got in at the same time via the builder category, based primarily on his design of the Glen Abbey Golf Club. Nicklaus had also been a strong supporter of the Canadian Open. He never did win it, although he finished second or tied for second seven times.

As for Moe's induction, Marlene Streit, a member of the Hall of Fame's inaugural class and of its selection committee, said, "He is in on his record. It speaks for itself. It's better than some and equal to all." Streit added that the RCGA had issues with Moe that "go back so long ago, to the way he handled himself and that trouble at the Masters."

She referred to the "good old boys" at the RCGA who were miffed because of the possibility that the Masters committee had stopped inviting Canadian Amateur winners to the tournament because Moe had walked off the course. That has never been proven, and Masters officials have consistently denied that was the reason. The Masters stopped inviting the winner of the previous year's Canadian Amateur in 1961.

I spoke with Moe the day after the announcement of his induction. He was working on his game. "It's nice and sunny today," he said from the pro shop at Royal Oak in Titusville, Florida, an hour by his usual slow drive from the motel room in which he lived. "I'm doing the same thing I always do. Why should I do anything different? I'm doing what I've done for thirty-five years." Hit golf balls, that is. "After all these years, I know the RCGA didn't put me in," Moe said. "The public did. The media did."

Bob Weeks, editor of *Score Magazine*, had written a strongly worded editorial in which he argued that Moe should be inducted on his record. Readers had sent him some sixty letters agreeing with him. I'd argued in many columns, including one after I returned from the PGA Teaching and Coaching Summit where Moe's appearance by video was so well received, that his induction was long overdue.

The announcement of his induction didn't impress Moe. "I didn't make speeches, I didn't dress up, I couldn't afford to," he said. "It was just my genes or my personality. I couldn't help it. But it's the way they [RCGA officials] are. I don't care one bit. I won't go to the dinner. If I did go, I'll say that the public forced them to get me in. I would say that right on the mike. I should have been in at forty-five, not sixty-five."

In late 2001, I called Karen Hewson, the curator of the RCGA Hall of Fame and Museum. I asked her what the RCGA had on file about Moe, particularly any information pertaining to his removal from the 1956 Americas Cup team. Marion Doherty, of course, had told me that the file Anglin had given her had gone missing. But maybe it had turned up in the fifteen years since she'd told me that. Karen did a thorough search but found nothing. "I wish I could find the file," she told me. "We don't have much before the 1970s." She figured that the RCGA must have left the files downtown on Bay Street in Toronto when the organization moved its headquarters in the mid-1970s from there to Golf House at Glen Abbey.

There the matter must rest. I still find it curious that nobody nominated Moe for so long. I myself could have nominated him. I don't know why I didn't. I never did look into the nomination procedure. I also wonder why Anglin, for one, or any RCGA governors who weren't on the Hall of Fame selection committee — a member can't make a nomination — didn't at least suggest that somebody nominate Moe. Anglin certainly respected him as a golfer. He was the referee in Moe's semi-final match at the 1956 Canadian Amateur in Edmundston, New Brunswick. Johnny Miles, who worked for *Sports Illustrated*, was his opponent. Anglin watched as Miles shot even par in the morning and finished eight holes down to Moe. Moe shot 64, eight under par. He won eight and seven; he was thirteen under par for the twenty-nine holes it took him to end the match. He beat Jerry Magee five and four the next day to win his second straight Canadian Amateur and earn another invitation to the Masters.

"That was the finest round I'd seen in a long time," Anglin once told me. "It was absolutely miraculous. I'd station myself behind Moe in line with the pin, and he never hit one more than six feet from the pin." Anglin and I were talking in 1986, thirty years after he'd exiled Moe from the America's Cup. The matter still bothered him. "It was a rough time," he said. "I was mainly criticized by Gordon Bowers, a past president of the RCGA. He asked what's going on when we have to find out from the newspapers [that Moe was selling his prizes for cash]. We had to act." Of Moe, Anglin told me, "I never knew if he was born retarded or not. He was certainly not a mature person." He added that Moe never seemed to hold anything against him. "We would say hello. We'd have a chat."

Although Moe had said he wouldn't show up at his induction, he did. Friends told many stories about Moe that hot summer evening at Foxwood. He was quiet as people spoke. My notes from the evening remind me that a chill went down my spine when Moe waved to the people gathered to celebrate his induction as he was introduced. Dinner was straight from Moe's menu; he asked that ribs and sausage be served. Jacques Nols, the Royal Canadian Golf Association president, remembered spending the summer of 1966 caddying on the Canadian Tour, then called the Peter Jackson Tour. "Moe was clearly the best player and the biggest attraction. People were amazed by the accuracy of his shots, the speed of his play and his spoken words. His ball striking ability was second to none. Moe became a legend. He remains a great player and he deserves to be in the Canadian Golf Hall of Fame."

Moe was holding a putter in his hands and drinking a Diet Coke. A toast to Moe was offered, and again he stood and gave a little wave of the hand. A short video was shown, which included Frank Sinatra singing "My Way." Moe was given a standing ovation when the video ended. He said quietly that his efforts were "a lot of hard work, a lot of hard work." He was about to make some remarks and asked that the lights be turned down. "I'm going to talk for an hour now," he said, smiling, and kidding. He was applauded, and then he spoke.

"To the Maue family, I can't thank them enough," he said. "They always treat me like a brother." He remembered playing Rockway when he was fourteen, and that "you were high man if you shot seventy." He said, "I always loved Moe Norman, I never kicked myself in the ass," and, "I put a different perspective on this game. I shot the fastest sixty-fives, two hours and ten minutes. I was a reindeer. You were all big mooses . . . I was the laughing stock of Canada, but here I am." A story was told during the evening about Walter Cunningham, a Scotsman who'd been the head professional at the London Hunt and Country Club. Cunningham had watched Moe play a round in which he never faced a putt more than six feet long. He remembered the accuracy with which Moe drove the ball. "In forty years, I've never seen the ball driven as well as that." How must it have been for Moe to do one thing surpassingly well, yet still think of himself as the country's laughing stock?

Gus Maue delivered the major address of the guests. "Moe is a special person. He's misunderstood. But he's the only guy I know who, when he hits the ball, and it doesn't matter where he's playing, everybody stops to watch him."

Moe had calmed down since receiving word of his induction. He still thought he ought to have been inducted twenty years earlier, but his voice had lost its edge. Maybe it was being at Foxwood, among friends, and maybe he allowed himself to feel accepted by people among whom he'd never felt comfortable.

"I know I'm not an outsider, that people here grew up like I did," Moe said of being at Foxwood, underscoring how much of an outsider he felt at clubs where he had played, and won, so many tournaments. "Being here brings good memories," Moe said, as the evening continued.

Nicklaus was inducted into the Canadian Golf Hall of Fame eleven days later, at Glen Abbey. Moe attended the ceremony and mingled in the crowded room at the cocktail party before the dinner. He was content. Speaking with him there, I had many mixed feelings. Moe should have been inducted so many years earlier. But at least he'd finally been inducted. I'd heard over the years that the RCGA would wait until he passed away before inducting him. But, thankfully, that didn't happen. Moe was now a member of the Canadian Golf Hall of Fame, on his record alone. He belonged there.

ON THE BACK NINE

TIGER WOODS WAS PRACTICING HIS putting at the Glen
Abbey Golf Club on the Tuesday of the 2000 Bell Canadian
Open. Moe was also on the green, thirty feet away. He
was watching Woods and other golfers. Clay Edwards, a
swing coach who lives in Houston and was working with
Richard Zokol, had been waiting for this moment. Who
knew when such a moment would come again?

Edwards walked over to Woods. "Tiger, Moe Norman
is over there. You have to meet him." Woods looked up and
walked over with Edwards to where Moe was standing.
"Tiger, I'd like you to meet Moe Norman," Edwards said.
Tiger and Moe exchanged glances, greeted one another
and shook hands firmly. Woods went back to continue

putting. Moe and Edwards chatted for a few minutes.

Later that day Woods was hitting balls on the range while Bob Vokey, the craftsman who makes wedges for Titleist that many tour players use, was standing beside him. Vokey was talking to Woods, who suddenly looked up and interrupted him. "Wait a minute, Bob, Moe's over there hitting balls. Let's watch him." Tom Lehman also stopped hitting balls.

"Tiger's there, Tom's there. They stop, and they just stand there, watching Moe," Vokey said.

Woods was impressed with Moe's swing. *Golf Digest's* Jaime Diaz interviewed him for a story published in January 2005. Woods told Diaz that only two golfers, Moe Norman and Ben Hogan, "owned their swing." Moe always said that he had "captured" his swing, meaning the same thing. His swing was as much a part of him as his arms. "I want to own mine," Woods added.

Three months later Woods won his fourth Masters. ESPN did a piece on him in which he again spoke about Moe. "He woke up every day knowing he was going to hit it well," Woods told Scott Van Pelt. "He just knew he was going to hit it well. Every day."

Woods likened the way Moe swung the golf club to the robotic ball-hitting machine called Iron Byron, named after Byron Nelson. Nelson won five major championships, and in 1945 he won eleven consecutive PGA Tour events. Inventor George Manning designed the robot at the request of the United States Golf Association, which was looking for a machine that would hit the ball the same way and same distance every time. Nelson was so consistent — about as robotic as a golfer could be — that the machine came to be dubbed Iron Byron. The USGA used it until 2000 to test balls and clubs for their conformity to equipment standards.

That's why, when Woods thought about Moe and spoke with Van Pelt, he said, "It's frightening how straight he hits it. It's like Iron Byron. The ball doesn't move."

•

WOODS PICKED UP ON A CENTRAL FACT of Moe's ball flight when he said that the ball doesn't move. That fact also intrigued Wally Uihlein when he decided in 1995 to provide Moe with $5,000 monthly for the rest of his life. Moe wasn't required to do anything in return. Why would a major company such as Titleist, which the multinational Fortune Brands then owned, make such a gesture? I called Uihlein in the late winter of 1995 after learning about his generous offer. "We just want to make sure that what doesn't happen thirty years from now is that Moe is forgotten about when people talk about the best players," he told me. "Our feeling is that Moe may be one of the top five human interest stories in the game. If you have cried about Ken Venturi playing the last thirty-six holes of the U.S. Open [in 1964, while he was suffering from heat exhaustion] and winning, how can you not help but cry when you hear Moe's story?"

Titleist continued to send the monthly check to Moe, as Uihlein promised, even as his life and his wanderings in the golf world slowed down. Moe blacked out on a highway

in southern Ontario in late September 1997, while returning from a clinic he'd given, and crashed into a guardrail.
His Cadillac was wrecked, but he emerged without injury
except for some bruising — or so it seemed. He walked
to the nearby Deer Ridge club the next morning. He was
worried and didn't know why he had blacked out. The pro
Ron Silver called Gus Maue. His wife, Audrey, picked up
Moe from church that Sunday morning. Tests determined
that Moe had blacked out because of a heart attack.

He was told he couldn't go to Florida, at least not right
then. Moe usually began driving there in late October.
Instead, one morning, he was at the Carlisle Golf and
Country Club with Nick Weslock. This was one of his golfing haunts, a public course where he felt comfortable. Moe
had lost eight or nine pounds in the month since his heart
attack, as I saw when I drove the hour or so from my home
in Toronto to meet him and Nick for breakfast. Moe missed
his usual bacon and eggs, which doctors had ordered him to
avoid. He was having a roast beef sandwich instead.

"No more ham and eggs," Moe said, eyeing Weslock's
bacon and eggs while patting his stomach. "No more bacon
and eggs. The yolk is bad for you. And I can't eat the skin on
chicken, or French fries and gravy. No more cheeseburgers,
either, or salt, or doughnuts. No apple pie and ice cream."

The food he loved wasn't all he would miss. Moe was
in despair because he couldn't go to Florida. "I'd be leaving
today or tomorrow. First time I'll see snow in forty-three
years. I'll go nuts next week when it gets dark at 5:30." The
clocks would be turned back an hour then. "What'll I do?"

Moe asked. He would be out of his routine. What would he do, indeed?

Moe was holding a putter as he spoke. I noticed that its flat end was on the forward side of the shaft, which is unusual. Most golfers who have a flat side on their grip ensure it's on top of the shaft so that their thumbs can run down it. But Moe had a reason for doing it his way.

"I'm left-handed," Moe said, who swung and putted right-handed. "This way the left hand [his stronger hand] won't twist. It puts the putter in the lifeline of your left hand, away from your fingers. What an advantage, what an advantage."

Fingers are fast, palms are calm. Moe's putter was his pacifier that morning at Carlisle. Moe wasn't calm, but he was soothed for the moment as he talked golf.

I left Carlisle and kept in touch with Moe through Nick and the Maues as he tried to adjust to life in the cold late fall and in the convalescent home. He was getting ready for bypass surgery in late November at University Hospital in London, Ontario. I got a call through to him in his hospital room before his surgery. "Everything has changed so much, everything, your thoughts, the things you see, it's all so different now," he told me wistfully.

Moe had learned that he wouldn't be allowed to drive after his surgery, not for six weeks at least. But he effectively lived in his car. He was as elusive as a hole-in-one, driving from course to course in southern Ontario, meandering south to Florida through Pinehurst, North Carolina. It was difficult to visualize Moe without a car, Moe in a room,

Moe frozen in place. Audrey Maue mentioned how difficult it would be for him without his car and that, sitting in his room and barred from the world outside, he wanted to know where his car was. The Maues parked it in front of the convalescent home so he'd know where it was.

The story of what Moe said when he awoke from his bypass surgery quickly became legend. A doctor asked him if he knew where he was. "Sure, on the third green," Moe said. Was he hallucinating? Moe insisted he was on the third green of the London Hunt and Country Club. The doctor did some research and learned that University Hospital was on the grounds of the original London Hunt and Country Club. Moe's room was in a part of the hospital on the site of the old third green.

After surgery, Moe was forced to spend the entire winter in Canada. He did, indeed, see snow for the first time in forty-three years.

•

WALLY UIHLEIN WAS ENGAGED IN A conversation with a colleague on the veranda at the back of Augusta National's clubhouse. It was the Tuesday of the 2011 Masters. His son Peter, the 2010 U.S. Amateur champion, had been invited to the Masters because of his win, and he was playing a practice round. I'd driven up to Augusta from Jupiter, where I'd been spending the winter annually since the mid-1990s. I knew that I'd run into Uihlein. It had been over fifteen years since he'd made his financial commitment to Moe and six and a half years since Moe's death. How, all these years later, did Uihlein see and understand Moe? Had he remained interested in him? I wanted to explore these questions with Uihlein and waited until he and his colleague had parted before I asked him if we could sit down. He led me to a small room inside the clubhouse, just past the players' dining area beside their locker room. The room was set aside during the Masters for Titleist representatives. Boxes of shoes and golf balls filled the floor space, but there was room for a desk and a couple of chairs.

Uihlein told me of the times he and his colleague Joe Turnesa, a Titleist salesman, showed up at the Canadian Open. This was in the 1970s and '80s at Glen Abbey. Titleist people were visible by the white sports coats they wore. They noticed players gathering on the range around one player in particular: Moe.

"I've seen only two players in the history of the game that other players would stop and watch on the range, Ben Hogan and Moe," Uihlein said. "Moe would time his appearance. He'd hold court on Tuesday or Wednesday."

Uihlein was taken with Moe and the interest he sparked in other players. Wasn't it impossible to hit a ball so straight, time after time? Where was the variation that goes with being a human being whose arms and legs can move in ways that aren't subject to conscious control? Moe was a trick-shot artist, except that he wasn't hitting trick shots. He was hitting call shots. "Okay, here's one knee-high, left to right. Here's one head-high, right to left."

Fred Couples had played a practice round one day during the Canadian Open when he wandered over to the practice range at Glen Abbey and saw Moe hitting balls. He watched for a while and said to his caddy, Joe LaCava, "Joe, I'm so jacked up I have to play another nine holes. Let's go." Couples never played more practice rounds than he needed to, nor did he spend hours on the range. But Moe got him moving.

"I'd watch Moe and ask myself, 'How does he do that?'" Uihlein said. "The golf swing is a Ferris wheel on a tilted angle. If you want the perfect shot, you want perfect side-spin — no sidespin, that is. Moe is the only golfer we ever tested who imparts no sidespin to the ball. He had backspin and rifle spin. That's the most efficient strike."

Craig Shankland had also used the Ferris wheel analogy. It's a common way of looking at the swing. What is uncommon is that a golfer can embody it exactly.

But for Uihlein there was more to Moe than his golf swing. Sure, he wanted to preserve his swing on film; he likened a film of his swing to the Zapruder film of John F. Kennedy's assassination in that he thought it would be studied down through generations of golfers. But he also wanted his industry to recognize Moe for who he was beyond his golf swing. As we spoke in that small room in the Augusta National clubhouse, while the world's famous golfers prepared for the Masters, Uihlein was emotional. His voice broke when he referred to Moe as an "industry outlier," somebody whom the industry hadn't recognized properly. He thought the equipment industry and the golf world at large had effectively discarded Moe because, after all, he hadn't won big tournaments. It was nearly forty years since Moe had walked off the Masters when Titleist gave him his monthly check. Uihlein said the equipment industry had a poor record of dealing with idiosyncratic golfers or "characters." He said the golf industry in the private sector is Darwinian.

So, of course, is the game. A professional golfer doesn't get a salary. He makes the cut in a tournament, or he doesn't make a cent. It's survival of the fittest, in the sports category. I'd seen the game chew up and spit out hundreds of golfers who on driving ranges around the world looked as if they could make a good living in tournaments. But something happens between the range and the course in tournaments. Something happened to Moe between Canadian tournament courses and American tournament courses.

Uihlein considered Moe a golfing savant lost to the industry. It was in that context, he said, that he wanted to do something for Moe. He told Gus Maue what he wanted to do, and Maue told Moe about what Uihlein termed an "industry scholarship on the back end of life." Moe asked Uihlein what he needed to do in return for the money. "I said, 'Just be yourself.'"

Titleist's parent company gave Uihlein some heat. He replayed the concerns to me. "What are you doing? You're doing this in perpetuity? Yes. Do you know what it will cost? Yes, but that's not what it's about."

Moe was given his back-end scholarship. Uihlein told Maue that he was Moe's local guardian and that Titleist was his industry guardian. Uihlein was concerned that younger golfers might forget about Moe, ignore what he had done and who he was, and disregard what his way of playing and being said about golf as an individual game. In their book *Play Your Best Golf Now*, Pia Nilsson and Lynn Marriott write, "One of the joyous things about golf is that it is a highly individualized sport, while at the same time being extremely social." Moe was the quintessential individual in the sport, but he struggled with its social nature. Uihlein was welcoming him into the fraternity after so many years. He didn't stop at the back-end scholarship either. In a way, Uihlein became Moe's public relations agent as he helped to bring his story to the world beyond golf swing aficionados. Years later, after I spoke with Uihlein at the Masters, Karen Gray, Titleist's supervisor of research and a golf pro, echoed his feelings about Moe. She'd seen Moe hit balls during testing and told me, "To this day I've never seen anything like it. I couldn't believe that he could hit shots with zero sidespin. You don't see *robots* with zero sidespin."

The annual PGA Merchandise Show in Orlando took place in late January 1995 in the massive Orange County Convention Centre. Paul DeCorso, a Titleist sales rep, introduced himself to Uihlein as the show ended. He thanked Uihlein for what he'd done for his wife, Sandy. Uihlein asked him what he meant and learned that Sandy DeCorso is Moe's niece; Moe's twin sister, Marie, is her mother. By providing Moe with the monthly check, Uihlein had also made his niece feel good and happy for Moe. She knew that Moe had been spurned over the years and that it had hurt him. I'd spoken from time to time with Marie and Sandy, who seemed to regret that Moe felt estranged from his family. They knew he was special, and they thought he deserved recognition and even celebration. Paul was simply telling Uihlein that, by giving Moe the back-end scholarship, he had not only assured wider acclaim for Moe but also made him feel that much more accepted.

Uihlein and his associates looked into Moe's background and story more deeply. Uihlein contacted his friend Jay Fitzgerald, then the executive director of *Golf Digest*, the game's most widely read magazine. He told Fitzgerald he thought that Moe was one of the great human interest stories in the game and that *Golf Digest* should do a story about him. This led to David Owen's mammoth cover story in the December 1995 issue.

Two months later Moe went to the 1996 PGA Merchandise Show with Maue. Uihlein had organized the filming of Moe's swing at the LPGA International Club in Daytona Beach, with Shankland supervising. Moe's swing had been shot from behind, or down the line to his target, face on and from above. Shankland had brought in a construction site boom. Moe's swing was being played in a loop on a giant screen in the convention center when Moe walked onto the floor with Maue. Moe, wearing what Uihlein described as a "kooky" sweater, stood there and looked up at the screen.

The moment was poignant, and there were tears in his eyes as Uihlein recalled it to me at Augusta National. "The picture of Moe standing there and watching himself really was worth a thousand words. From a metaphorical point of view, all the other stuff [the monthly payment to Moe, the articles written about him] didn't resonate. But this did. Moe just kept looking at the screen."

He embodied the spirit of Shivas Irons in Michael Murphy's book *Golf in the Kingdom*. Murphy's character was a mystical figure who held the secrets of the game in his soul and whose wisdom was of a different kind than golf professionals usually offer. "Fascination is the true and proper mother of discipline," Shivas says at a gathering of friends. "And gowf is a place to practice fascination. 'Tis slow enough to concentrate the mind and complex enough to require our many parts."

Moe never used such flowery language, but he did have a way with words. "Don't force it, finesse it. Stabilize, energize, contain, release." Or, "My way takes time, but it's the way to greatness. You have to taste victory and want it. If you can't taste victory, you won't get it." But how does a golfer "concentrate the mind"? How does a golfer "taste victory"? Moe also said, "Golf is intoxication without the alcohol. It cleanses the mind and rejuvenates the body. Some say it's a boy's game, but it builds men." Maybe these words weren't original with him, but he recited them so frequently they became his mantra.

Shivas and Moe did have their differences. Moe never drank alcohol; Shivas Irons did. More importantly, Shivas was a fictional creation; Moe was real. "Shivas Irons lives," Uihlein said of Moe. "He was someone who transcended just being a player."

As I listened to Uihlein, and as the Tuesday practice rounds at the Masters proceeded, I thought he was still trying to keep Moe alive and present. He kept the canister of film he'd taken of Moe's swing on a corner of his desk. He looked back in his mind's eye to when he'd offered Moe the monthly payment of $5,000, and it was apparent he thought that a generation of golfers was growing up and perhaps losing sight of Moe. "Moe was almost in a gulag. I'd ask if anybody had seen him lately, or heard of him, especially the forty-five-and-under generation. If you grew up in the industry, Moe's story was a little bit like *The Legend of Sleepy Hollow*. Does he really exist? Here he is, making his way up the coast from Florida. Maybe you saw him in Pinehurst or here and there. It's almost a reverse Swans of Capistrano." The cliff swallows returned to Capistrano every year by March 19th, or so the legend of the birds has it. Moe returned to Canada every spring, meandering along highways and back roads at slow speeds — the wandering golfer. He was no legend. Moe Norman lives, Uihlein said. Shivas Irons lives.

•

MOE'S HEART WAS FAILING. Nick Weslock met Moe on a cold day in late October 2003 at the Century Pines Golf Club near Hamilton, but Moe shouldn't even have been there. He wasn't supposed to be driving. He had suffered a stroke a month and a half earlier when he was at the Rockway club. He'd been taken by ambulance to the hospital. A valve in his heart was leaking, and then he contracted pneumonia. "I'm dying," he told Weslock. "But I don't care. I've had a great life."

By late summer 2004, Moe had lost so much weight he looked like half of himself. *Golf Digest* writer Guy Yocom had visited him for a question-and-answer session. Moe looked deathly ill in the photos that accompanied the piece; he was as thin as a one-iron. He was living at the Terrace on the Square retirement home in Waterloo and had breakfast with Weslock every morning.

Gus and Audrey Maue saw Moe on Thursday September 2, 2004, and that night Gus again visited him. He returned the next evening after meeting with Moe's doctor, and he found Moe in the dining hall eating ice cream. Moe was upset when Gus informed him that the police were going to take away his driver's licence. Moe asked, "What about a bicycle?" Gus told him that it wasn't possible for Moe to bike from where he was living to Rockway, so Moe then asked, "What about the trolley?" Gus told him that was perfect, because the bus went right by the retirement home, but that he wouldn't need it. Gus had lined up a full-time chauffeur for Moe, a fellow Moe knew from the local pool hall. He would be on call all the time. Moe cheered up at this news because he would still be able to make his rounds from course to course and, especially, to Rockway. Moe had stopped by the course regularly that summer. Rockway was home. It had provided him with sanctuary and a place to develop his game.

But his heart was wearing out. Moe had been up for a few hours when he sat down in a chair and asked the night watchman to call an ambulance. Moe first walked out to his car and was back in the building by the time he was picked up at 2 a.m. Saturday and taken to the hospital. Gus arrived at twenty minutes to four. The doctors were working on Moe's heart. His heart gave out for the last time, and Moe died at four in the morning. Marie was contacted that morning, as were his brothers Ron and Rick and his sister Doreen, a nun in Kenora. His sister Shirley was contacted in Edmonton and left to join the family.

Moe's friend Irv Lightstone, who'd gone to the 1956 Masters with Moe, had just come off the course at The Briars in Jackson's Point, Ontario, when his son told him that Moe had died. "We logged so many miles together," Irv told me. "Moe was a little boy in a man's body. That little boy was a little boy for a lifetime. But if you needed a friend, he was there. I don't know how he would have made it without Gus and Audrey." Irv remembered how much Conn Smythe had loved Moe. "He loved that maverick. He never called him Moe either. It was always Murray."

Moe had wanted Gus to take him to the Canadian Open, but he died a few days before the Tuesday when they would have gone. He'd asked Gus a few times if they could go. He'd wanted to make his annual visit to the tournament and, inevitably, to the practice range.

On the day that Moe died, Gus told me that at least he'd had some good years since his bypass surgery in November 1997. Gus thought that Moe had softened considerably in his last couple of years and was no longer brusque with people. He hadn't competed for a few years and thought people were showing him compassion. He'd also been in and out of the hospital so often and seen people suffer.

I spoke with Lorie Kane, Charlottetown's LPGA Tour player who had won four tournaments there, on the Saturday Moe died. "I'm crushed," Lorie told me. She was glad she'd seen him during the CN Canadian Women's Open in Niagara Falls the previous month. He had given her a lesson. "He made it so simple," Lorie recalled. She told me of the time they shared at Royal Oak every winter. She was living nearby and often met Moe at the club. "Thank God he had Gus and Audrey," Lorie said. "I watched Moe around a lot of people, and he had a radar sense of who he wanted to be around. I could understand what he taught me. It was very natural. He just had a sense of how a golf ball should be hit."

Gus was asked to go through Moe's belongings. It wasn't surprising to him when he found a Titleist ball and a few tees in the pants Moe was wearing when he was taken to the hospital for the last time. He also found his room key there, but no cash. Back at Moe's room, Gus looked through some seventy pairs of pants in Moe's room, but still found no cash. He located the keys to Moe's Cadillac in the room. The trunk of his car was jammed with more than 1,000 Titleist Pro V1 balls, a few sets of irons and ten pairs of golf shoes. Moe had also squirreled away some $20,000 in cash. He had never trusted banks.

Because I was caddying at the Canadian Open, I couldn't attend Moe's funeral on the Friday after his death. Gus and Audrey handled the details of the funeral, held at Saint Louis (Roman Catholic) Church in Waterloo. Some 600 people attended the funeral. Moe lay in an open coffin, a Titleist driver in his hands, wearing two watches and a bright sweater that dazzled with its colors. A putter had been placed in each of the coffin's four corners. A black visor that he'd worn was there, along with a can of Diet Coke, his golf bag and a pair of the alligator shoes he'd loved. The photo of Moe hitting balls at the National while Nick Price, Nick Faldo, Fred Couples and Ben Crenshaw watched was there.

Audrey and Moe's niece Sandy DeCorso spoke at the funeral. Wayne Gretzky's father, Walter, who'd known Moe for fifteen years, was one of the pallbearers, as was Mike Martz, Moe's great pal and fellow pro. He wore one of Moe's black-and-white checkerboard sports jackets. Jimmy Laflamme, the boy who was tobogganing with Moe when Homer Berner's car hit them, attended the funeral. A traditional poem called "I'm Free" was given to those who attended the funeral. It had been altered to read, in part, "I could not stay another day / To laugh, to love, to golf or play."

Three times as many people as Gus had thought would attend showed up. Rob Strahan, the head pro at Westmount, slipped out of the church to call the club and ask that enough food be set out at the reception. Four hundred people went to Westmount. The Golf Channel was there.

I wrote a couple of articles about Moe the week after he died, and many readers wrote to me. One reader remembered watching Moe give a clinic at the Muskoka Lakes Golf and Country Club. A fellow asked Moe if he could hit a draw and then a fade. Moe said, "Yes, I can, but why would I, I can hit it straight." Another reader remembered asking Moe why he never practiced out of sand traps. "Why would I? I hit the ball in the fairway." This particular reader wrote, "It was easy to laugh at Moe's traits. Who knew that his simple approach to golf and life held a good many lessons for all of us? I wish I knew him."

I was in love with golf. I was married to hitting a golf ball.
I'm not sorry. What a great feeling, hitting it straight and solid
for over thirty-five years. — Moe, 1986

Elegy for Moe

MOE'S YOUNGEST BROTHER RICHARD lives with his wife in a
small house across from a community center in Kitchener.
Two metal putting cups on the floor of the front room announce that a golfer lives here. A putter leans against a wall.
The Titleist golf bag that was filled with Moe's clubs at his
funeral stands on its own, with a couple of clubs inside.

On the day I visited, in June 2011, Richard showed me
one of the Titleist drivers that Moe had used. Lead tape
thickened the club's soleplate. Richard also showed me
some of the Adams Tight Lies irons that Moe had once
used. I swung the seven-iron back and forth, feeling the
tire-like, thick rubber Goodwin grip that Moe had favored.
The grip was so tacky it was as if there was glue on the

rubber. I examined some of the other irons and noticed that Moe had shaved every one but the nine-iron and wedge on the bottom of the blade's leading edge.

Barney Adams, the founder of Adams Golf, had made these irons for Moe. They met when Barney, who lived in Dallas, came to Royal Oak in Titusville to meet his mother. She lived in a home on the course. Barney watched Moe hit balls every day and sometimes played nine holes with him in the evening. "Or, more correctly, I was allowed to be there," Barney advised me. "Moe played his own game, two balls on every shot, and his goal was to shoot par or better." This game is called "worst ball." Say the player hits a ball four feet from the hole. He then hits a second ball, and it buries under the lip in a bunker. By the terms of the game, he must play the worst of the two balls. If he then plays a miraculous shot from under the lip to within three feet of the hole, well, he must still hit a second shot from under the lip. George Knudson used to say that no golfer should consider trying to make a living as a tour golfer unless he can shoot par or better playing worst ball. "As any gambler knows, this should be impossible," Barney said. "But Moe did it more often than not."

As they got to know each other, Moe confided in Barney that he didn't like the irons he was using. Barney realized the problem was that they were too light. However, as he said, "They weren't really light, but they were too light by Moe's standards. Moe was strong, and not just strong but almost freakily strong, which was one of the reasons I never felt an ordinary person could emulate his swing." I thought of the times that Moe, in his playful and friendly way, would greet me by pinching my cheek. But he'd pinch it so hard that it hurt and often left a red mark.

A normal five-iron, Barney informed me, weighs about 250 grams. He figured that Moe wanted his five-iron closer to 275 to 280 grams. "Off the charts in the clubmaking world," Barney said. But Moe wanted clubs that heavy. I knew he liked a club that was less a matchstick than an oak tree but didn't realize how heavy one of his clubs felt until I held one in my hands that day in Richard's house. How had Barney made such a heavy club?

Barney used a mixture of tungsten powder, epoxy and lead tape to get the weight as close as possible to what Moe wanted. Then he had to work on the grip as a counterbalance to the head weight. He made the grip thick and used the heaviest and stiffest shafts he could find and bent them two degrees flat from standard. Barney presented Moe with a set from three-iron through pitching wedge. This was during a period when clubs were getting lighter and lighter. "They have their place, but with Moe and other great ball strikers I've always gravitated to heavier clubs," Barney said, and even as he approached seventy he used heavier clubs due to Moe's influence. "One lesson I took from Moe was not to get carried away with light clubs," he said.

I had come out from Toronto to see Richard in the early afternoon, following his early morning round of golf. Richard had retired at sixty-three from his job as a long-distance truck driver and had since played golf every morning from when the courses in his area open in early spring to when they close in late autumn or, sometimes, early winter. "I'm addicted," Richard said, who walks every round except when forced to ride. "Don't interfere with my golf game. I play seven days a week, even in bad weather. People ask me how often I play, and I ask them when the courses open and when they close. I play every day in between." His handicap is three, although he says he's had the putting yips for three years. His practice stroke is perfect, but then he flinches when he makes the stroke that matters. What else is new? Richard hit eight greens in regulation the other day on his front nine and three-putted six times. Still, he knows the game. He caddied regularly at Westmount and for long-hitting Mike Souchak in the 1957 Canadian Open at Westmount. Moe played that Canadian Open. People who knew Richard was Moe's brother called him "Little Moe."

Richard speaks with the help of an electronic prosthesis implanted in his throat. He was diagnosed with throat cancer in 2000 and had his voice box removed. He's had a heart attack and recently might have suffered a small stroke. He was seeing double during a round of golf the other day and wondered which ball he should hit. He will see a neurologist soon. Meanwhile, he plays golf every day and sometimes alone. Once a year he plays alone with Moe's clubs. "That's me, being Moe," Richard said. "That's my game with Moe."

Moe baffled Richard, as he did every member in the family. Richard doesn't know why Moe felt so alienated from his immediate family or why he said his parents and siblings refused to watch him play golf. Richard and his dad took the bus to Rockway to watch Moe, but he avoided them. A family gathering was held in 1999 at the Bohemian Restaurant in Waterdown, Ontario, to celebrate Moe's sister, and Sister, Doreen's fifty years as a nun. Richard and his siblings were shocked when Moe pulled up in the parking lot with Mike Martz. Moe's twin sister, Marie, told the writer John Gordon that the family hadn't seen him since a tournament in Hamilton fifty years before but that an invitation had still been sent to him. She told a friend, "If you see two moons up in that sky, that's the time we'll see Moe here. Well, there weren't two moons, but there was Moe, sure enough."

Everybody greeted Moe warmly when he emerged from his Cadillac. He hadn't attended a family function in those fifty years, and his nieces and nephews had never met their uncle. Richard remembers that Moe didn't spend much time with his siblings, although he did chat with his many nieces and nephews; his will stipulated that the considerable proceeds from his estate be divided equally among them. At the reunion, Moe handed a club from a new signature line with his name on them to an eight-year-old great-niece and a ten-year-old great-nephew. As always, he was comfortable with children but not with adults. He allowed himself to be part of a family photo, had dinner with everybody and then went on his way into the southern Ontario countryside. He'd evidently mellowed to some degree when it came to his family. Maybe he knew his life was winding down after his heart attack a couple of years earlier. It's impossible to know. Moe, who would turn seventy a couple of months later, never did explain why he showed up at the family gathering.

"He did live his way," Richard told me. "I guess that's what is so fascinating about him. Where did he get all that talent? The family is sure his accident did something and that it explains everything about him. To me, he played with a terrible swing, but he made it work. Moe lived for golf. Golf was his salvation."

•

IT'S LATE JULY, TWO DAYS AFTER THE 2011 Canadian Open has ended in Vancouver. I'm sitting on the deck beside The Hideout, a yurt that is the halfway house at the Sagebrush Golf and Sporting Club in British Columbia's Nicola Valley. I'm thinking about freedom and expressing oneself while pursuing what one enjoys and finds the most fulfilling. In Moe's case, that was hitting a golf ball. If Moe didn't need to eat and sleep, he would have spent twenty-four hours a day doing that.

I drove out to Sagebrush with Dick Zokol the day after the Canadian Open ended in Vancouver. Sagebrush was Zokol's dream, his vision. I'm surrounded by the course, which he designed with Rod Whitman and Armen Suny. The course was seven years in the dreaming and the making and opened two years earlier. I was last here in the summer of 2008, before it opened the following spring. The thirteenth hole near where I'm sitting plays past a corner of a pond where golfers fly-fish. The hole was complete when I was here for the first time, and we played the short par-four from the high tee behind me. We hit a variety of shots into the green. We played some along the ground, bouncing the ball off slopes toward the pin. We played a few shots in the air, carrying the ball back toward the hole. The situation presented many options, and we were called upon to hit the shot with which we felt the most comfortable and believed best suited what was in front of us.

I drove the three hours from busy Vancouver here with Dick because I was looking for a peaceful place after the hectic Canadian Open. I'd walked the tree-lined, narrow fairways of the Shaughnessy Golf and Country Club during the tournament and on the final day had followed Adam Hadwin, a twenty-three-year-old professional from Abbotsford, an hour east of Vancouver.

Hadwin was the low Canadian at the 2010 Canadian Open in Toronto, and he qualified for and played solid golf in the U.S. Open, a month before coming to Shaughnessy. He started the last round two shots behind the leader and was playing in the last group in his national championship. He had won twice on the Canadian Tour, but this was a big step up. He demonstrated a penchant for being the center of attention. Still, he acknowledged the evening before the final round that he wasn't even a PGA Tour player. That was true: he wasn't a PGA Tour member, had no status there and entered the Canadian Open on the strength of a sponsor's exemption.

Nevertheless, Hadwin was playing with both control and abandon. He merged the two after four-putting the eighth green for a double bogey and then bogeying the eleventh hole. But then he birdied three of the last seven holes to tie for fourth place. With his jet-black hair, and wearing sunglasses, white slacks and a red shirt (Canadian colors), Hadwin walked up the final fairway to a standing ovation that started 150 yards from the green. He raised one arm and then the other. Hadwin had more than a little swagger and was turning into a rock star — golf variety — that late afternoon under a baby-blue sky, sunshine and warm temperatures. Some golfers welcome the spotlight and feed off its heat and energy. Moe wasn't inclined in that direction. But he did play with control and abandon as he moved along in his bubble. And he played with freedom, because he occupied that bubble, especially when he was on a driving range, giving a clinic or playing with friends. The bubble he occupied didn't allow disturbances, though, which is why, I think, he couldn't cope with the game's public demands.

To me, golf at its best is an adventure and an exercise in freedom. Moe was a loner who found the perfect game for himself, and in it he found perfect moments.

Moe would have been happy to be at Sagebrush with Zokol and me. We were using six clubs each, for the sheer pleasure of having to be inventive. We were far from the mechanistic world of modern professional golf, with its insistence on video cameras that break down the swing into isolated segments, and its emphasis on the latest driver that supposedly hits the ball 300 yards and more, and golfers' reliance on global positioning systems so they can get precise yardages for themselves. Golf, one of the quintessential games of self-reliance, has gradually and inexorably moved to where players are dependent on outside agencies. Tour pros travel with an entourage that includes swing and mental coaches, nutritionists and physical trainers. Jack Nicklaus said that his instructor, Jack Grout (golfers had "instructors" in Nicklaus's time, not "coaches"), not once was on the practice tee with him during a tournament. They met at the start of each year to review the fundamentals, and that was it. Nowadays, the practice tee at tournaments is so crowded one can hardly move. There's no freedom when so many eyeballs and so many "experts" are scrutinizing every move and examining every thought.

When Moe was inducted into the Canadian Golf Hall of Fame, I stood with him on a patio of the Foxwood Golf Club. He stood there for a moment gazing out over the holes. He was quiet. I was quiet. There was peace out there and freedom. Moe was at home, while the guests at his induction milled inside and enjoyed cocktails and conversation before the formal ceremony inducting Moe got under way. I had the feeling Moe would have been happy to stand there for a long time.

At Shaughnessy, Hadwin did play with freedom. His swing coach, Brett Saunders, was caddying for him, but he didn't use a mental coach, not yet anyway. (He did add one to his team a few days after the Canadian Open.) Hadwin hit his tee shot on the par-four sixteenth hole just into the right rough and reviewed his next shot with Saunders, who said, "128 front, 153 total," advising Hadwin of the yardage to the front of the green and to the hole.

"What will it play, sixty?" Hadwin asked, trying to assess the effect of the gentle breeze.

"If it jumps [from the rough], more like sixty," Saunders answered, agreeing with Hadwin's assessment.

Hadwin replied, "You like nine? Nine will cover the front."

Saunders agreed that a nine-iron would get Hadwin's ball at least over a bunker short of the green and to the front. Hadwin committed to his shot, took his club back until the shaft was parallel to the ground in his pre-shot waggle and swung.

"First cut," Saunders said.

The ball finished just short of pin-high in the first cut of rough to the right of the green. Hadwin walked to his ball and played briskly when it was his turn. He chipped within six feet of the hole, made the par putt and parred the last two holes in front of the partisan crowd. It was hard to avoid the feeling that this was a coming-out party, the excitement was so high. But, as Hadwin cautioned later, he knew he couldn't build a career on one tournament. Still, it was an impressive start. Who knew where his career would go from there?

I bring this up as I sit at The Hideout because I hope Hadwin will continue to play with abandon, allow himself to, well, be himself, even as the people who want to make money off him begin to circle. He played beautifully, and I hope he will retain his craving for hitting pure golf shots. How will he handle the attention from the business world?

Will he continue to simply *play* golf, to do what brought him to this point?

Moe did continue to *play* golf after he was the same age as Hadwin. He wasn't a professional at that age and still had his 1955 and 1956 Canadian Amateur championships ahead. He was moving into the higher reaches of Canadian golf and, inevitably, on to life as a tour pro. Moe was not fit for that life, but he tried it, over and over again. It always amazed me that he was able to continue deriving joy from hitting golf balls while the commercial aspects of the game and the officials who run it could easily have suffocated him.

Moe knew he could find perfect moments away from the world of professional tournaments, and he left that world behind easily after every event he played. He changed his shoes by the trunk of his car, put his clubs away and drove off. He found solace at the range or with his friends at Brantford during their regular games. He found comfort every spring when he returned home, quickly going to Brantford, filling his tour bag with golf balls and walking the course on his own. This was Moe's way of training for the Canadian golf season. He couldn't often walk courses in Florida because that's usually not allowed. Moe had to use a golf cart. Back at Brantford, he walked and carried his heavy bag. This was not a burden to him. He was the same man who'd wanted to carry his own clubs during that 1956 Masters. You don't do that at the Masters, but, really, why not? The rule made no sense to Moe. The rule had nothing to do with playing the game. It had to do with what was deemed proper. Moe wanted to carry his own clubs. To do otherwise constrained his freedom.

Just as I had thought about Moe when I was caddying for Zokol in the 2004 Canadian Open, I thought of him while playing Sagebrush that morning with six clubs. What freedom, what pleasure, to use a limited set on an immense, open landscape — to play with abandon. If I had limited the number of clubs I would use, I had expanded my scope in this big sky country, overlooking Nicola Lake, with mountains all around. Many people questioned his sanity when Zokol decided in 2002 to build a course here. The elevation changes 300 feet from the course's lowest point. How could he even think of building a course on what is really a hillside? But Zokol envisaged golf in these wide-open spaces where deer, osprey, bald eagles and red-tailed hawks are often seen. He walked out one day from The Hideout and saw a black bear a few feet away. Zokol stood silently, looking at the bear. He picked up a chunk of rock and threw it hard on the ground. The bear turned and walked into the woods.

Moe would have enjoyed so much about Sagebrush. He would have played all day and until the sun set. He would have been set free to hit a fascinating variety of shots.

Zokol appreciated Moe. He and Clay Edwards were often the ones to encourage Moe to come out onto the range during a Canadian Open. "We'd spot him and bring him out while I hit balls," Zokol said. "We wouldn't ask him to hit balls, but at some point I'd just hand him one of my clubs, and he'd slide into my place with the flow of it.

He'd start hitting balls, and other players would come by and watch."

Moe made a point of watching Zokol when he tried to qualify in 1983 for the next year's PGA Tour. The six-round qualifying school took place at the Tournament Players Club's Stadium course in Ponte Vedra, Florida. From 100 yards away, Moe watched every shot Zokol hit for the six rounds. Zokol knew who Moe was but hadn't met him. Moe simply wanted to check out the young man who'd won the 1981 Canadian Amateur championship. Zokol tied for fifth and qualified for the PGA Tour. "I felt proud that Moe was there watching me," Zokol told me.

Nearly thirty years later Zokol and I were talking about being result oriented while playing rather than being fully engaged in the shot at hand. Zokol had asked Moe at the 1999 Canadian Open if he ever thought about his score while he was playing. "Never, never," Moe had answered. "Never get ahead of yourself. If you did that while you were driving, you'd crash."

Here, at Sagebrush, I found myself detached from my score while playing with six clubs. I'd entered Moe's world, a world in which I was immersed in the shot at hand. I felt long through the ball, my clubface extending toward my target. My swing felt larger, expanded, connected to that target. Moe used to tell me, "Shake hands with the flagstick." I was doing that. I was channeling Moe.

The week before, I'd spoken at Zokol's induction into the Canadian Golf Hall of Fame. The ceremony had taken place at the Marine Drive Golf Club, just up the road from

Shaughnessy. Zokol had grown up in a house on top of the hill, close to the course. He'd learned to play there while hitting balls and carrying his clubs around the course on summer evenings. Golf had helped him to mature. He is the first to admit that there was a time when he was running with the wrong crowd. His father, Joe, had put the brakes on that, and Zokol had taken to the course. He'd learned self-discipline and self-reliance.

That night at Marine Drive Zokol related the story of how he'd met Edwards, the instructor who would help him believe in himself and refine his swing. Zokol spoke of the time at the 1984 Bay Hill Classic in Orlando when he was hitting balls the day before the first round while Moe and another fellow he didn't know were standing nearby and watching him. He was hitting the ball terribly and asked Moe for some advice.

Moe turned to his side. "This guy can help you, this guy can help you," he told Zokol and pointed to Edwards.

Zokol wasn't interested in hearing from anybody but Moe, but before he could say anything Edwards was at his side. "I didn't want to be rude to him and decline, because Moe said he could help me. I was hitting three-irons, and the first thing Clay said to me was 'In your next swing, I want you to stress the shaft and compress the ball down the line as long as you can.' With those words in mind, I hit my next three-iron shot and had that 'feeling of greatness,' as Moe would have described it. That was the start of the close relationship I had with Clay. The next week I flew to Victoria, Texas, to work with Clay. I spent the week with him, and it was a turning point in my career. Later that year I finished fifth at the Canadian Open."

All his life Moe had done what Edwards suggested to Dick. I'd usually failed to notice because, like many other observers, I'd been too caught up in the peculiarities of his setup: how far he stood from the ball, his wide stance. These elements contributed to his precision, but it was the strike on the ball that was the guts of the matter. Moe once showed some black-and-white photos of his pre-impact position to a friend. The photos showed that Moe was so deep into the shot as he stressed the shaft that his right ankle was almost touching the ground. That's compressing the shaft. Moe was so strong that he could release the club through impact from there and then extend to the sky. It would have been a treat to see him extend to the big sky here at Sagebrush. That would have made some photograph or some painting. Still life with Moe, exploding through the ball. The picture, if it existed, would belong on the wall in The Hideout.

I extended farther through the ball, I believe, than I had in years, perhaps ever, as I played with Zokol. I remember a shot on the fourteenth hole when I was about 230 yards from the green — a rough estimate because I was playing by feel, not by a yardage book or GPS. I rarely hit the ball that far anymore even with my driver, and it's not age that has shortened my drives. I was swinging in too enclosed a space. I was swinging as if I were in a telephone booth or elevator. That seemed ridiculous in Sagebrush's enormous space. Meanwhile, I kept seeing Moe out there reaching to the sky. Zokol encouraged me to stress the shaft and compress the ball as far down the line as I could.

At home, I usually carry nine clubs so that I can walk. I play with more freedom than with fourteen clubs. I carry a driver, a three-wood, three-, five-, seven- and nine-irons, a wedge, a sand wedge and a putter. My six-club complement at Sagebrush — and they weren't even my own clubs — consisted of a driver, three-, five-, seven- and nine-irons and a putter. I chose a three-iron for my shot of 230 yards and thought only of going deep through the ball, stressing the shaft, compressing the ball and extending. I felt as if the ball were sticking to the face as I extended. I had no sensation of a hit; I was only swinging and squeezing that ball. When I looked up and held my position, in balance, the ball was flying toward the right center of the green, exactly where I'd aimed it. The ball carried about 215 yards and rolled up to pin-high. Thank you, Moe.

"Moe would like it here so much," I said to Zokol then.

He replied, "Nobody would be here to laugh at him. He'd be free. Freedom, that's what he wants."

I think that's all Moe ever wanted. That thought makes me happy, for the times he had it. He didn't always have it, but that wasn't because the game hurt him. Its conventions drained him. Moe was not confrontational. He was, in my experience, a gentle soul. George Knudson was right when he told me in my early days of writing that Moe was the most sensitive golfer I'd meet. Moe wanted only to hit golf balls and to play golf, really *play* it. Sagebrushian, I think. He was performing, but it didn't matter whether he was performing for anybody else — certainly not in a tournament. Hitting balls at a range and giving clinics were different matters. He hit balls one after the other. These were performances in two ways: because he was performing his art, and because others were watching him do it. Isn't one condition of a "performance" that observers are present?

Moe, in my view, was the Glenn Gould of golf. Each had his quirks, and people often commented on these quirks more than on their genius at their respective crafts. Gould wore gloves to protect his hands, even on hot days, while Moe wore turtlenecks in July to avoid sunburn. Each didn't like the bigger stage, where the golfer had to perform in front of people in a tournament and the pianist had to perform in front of people in the concert hall. Gould eventually rejected the concert hall and turned to the recording studio instead. But there's no equivalent in golf of the recording studio, to which Gould, one of the world's most well-known and most-studied pianists, then only thirty-one, retreated after his last public performance on April 10, 1964, in Los Angeles. Moe couldn't exactly put on an exhibition at a driving range or play a casual game with friends and have that count as a tournament round.

Gould thought the very idea of piano competitions was absurd. He performed in the studio, and only in the studio, once he left the stage. It was obvious to me that Moe didn't like competing with others. As he told Zokol, he never thought of results or outcomes. That wasn't entirely true, of course, because he did get nervous when in contention to win the 1963 Canadian Open, which led to his all but giving up during the back nine. He got stage fright, and he was forever deemed a loser by the golf world at large because he couldn't win on the biggest stages. Moe didn't want to be on the course in a tournament in the same way that Gould didn't want to be in a concert hall when he was performing. For Moe, practice was as authentic as the real thing or what others thought of as the real thing — a tournament. The real thing to Moe was hitting golf balls. I sometimes wonder what the golf world has lost by not having a library of films taken while Moe played golf alone or with friends. Wouldn't each round be a composition? We have Gould's recorded performances, many from the studio alone, some from his concert appearances. For Moe, every round was an edifice he built shot by shot, because he wasn't thinking of outcome or playing for score. He was conducting himself around the course. His sole concern was to play the correct shot, to hit the right note, for the situation at hand. He felt what to do instinctively, and he did it.

Moe belonged and thrived in the open spaces, hitting golf balls, walking from shot to shot, hole to hole. The game gave him the gift and consolation of freedom, yet it also restricted and confined him. It provided comfort to a man insecure in the wider world yet secure in his ability to make a golf ball do what he meant it to do. In a similar way, Gould was at home in open country, and he recorded three hour-long documentaries under the title of the Solitude Trilogy. *The Idea of North* was the most well known of the three documentaries. Gould was attracted to the idea of withdrawing from the world to achieve purity in his life and, thereby, his art.

Moe in effect withdrew from the world, or felt as if he did, when he hit golf balls. Golf protected him from the confusion of life beyond the driving range and the course. It was insulation, and perhaps it saved him. Who knows what he'd have done, or been, had he not latched on to the game? Would he have been homeless? It's possible. So, yes, golf did save him. But it also scarred him. It also wounded him. He felt the eyes of the golf authorities, the public and the media staring at and judging him.

•

AFTER PLAYING SAGEBRUSH WITH ZOKOL, I returned to the nearby Quilchena Hotel, where we were staying. Zokol and I had dinner with his associates Don Harvey and Terry Donald. During dinner, we enjoyed a couple of bottles of cabernet sauvignon from the BC winery Burrowing Owl. We talked about the pleasures of the game — a game that truly can be a hideout and a hideaway, a retreat. It was that for Moe, and, I have come to understand, that is one of its most important elements for me. I am fortunate to write about golf for my living, and doing so has taken me all over the world. It led me to Zokol, one of my closest friends. I won't forget his induction at Marine Drive or the two days we shared at Sagebrush. I won't forget the compassion that Zokol, who described himself as a "journeyman" golfer who won on the PGA Tour by hard work, showed for Moe. Zokol never laughed at Moe. He respected him. Two individuals making their way in the most individual of games.

After dinner, I returned to my room, turned on my computer and started up my music library. I listened to some of Ryan Bingham's lonely but somehow uplifting music — my wife would call him a GVG or gravelly voiced guy — and then I clicked on Gould's rendition of Bach's *Goldberg Variations*. While listening, I continued reading a book I'd been reading for a while, George Leroux's *Partita for Glenn Gould: An Inquiry into the Nature of Genius*. Leroux is a professor emeritus in the Department of Philosophy at the University of Quebec in Montreal. He started to write about Gould in 1987, and in his book, published in 2010, he says, "As a child the pianist already knew that his art could transport him to a rarefied and exclusive world" and that Gould experienced an "inner rapture" while playing.

Leroux could have been writing about Moe.

•

AFTER VISITING MOE'S BROTHER RICHARD at his home, I drove a short distance to Memory Gardens in Breslau. Moe is buried there. "It's a lovely monument," a lady in the office told me before directing me to his gravesite, a couple of hundred yards away in the only section of what are called "uprights." The black monument was easy to spot. It reads "MOE, a Canadian Legend." He's depicted in an image at the bottom left of the monument, at the finish of his swing, his hands high and stretched, the clubhead extended to the sky, with a bunker, a green and trees behind. Two golf balls, a Pinnacle and a Top-Flite, rested on a bottom ledge of the monument, while two others had been placed on the ground. Somebody had left a black-and-white photo of Moe smiling.

I stayed for a few minutes on the sunny, hot day. Birds were singing in the trees fifty yards behind the area where Moe is buried. I went to the trunk of my car and took a Titleist Pro V1 ball out of my golf bag. A logo read "George Knudson, Oakdale Pro-Am, Sept. 9th, 2008." The tournament raised money for cancer research at Toronto's Mount Sinai Hospital, in Knudson's memory. The logo included an image of Knudson, a golfer and fellow Canadian for whom Moe had a deep respect, and the feeling was mutual. The image depicted Knudson at the finish of his swing, looking at the target. I left the ball on Moe's gravestone.

Leaving the cemetery, I soon turned onto a country road, and in a moment I came to the Beaverdale Golf and Country Club on my left. Two youngsters were coming off a green. They were walking and carrying their golf bags to the next tee. A sign said "SteakNite Fridays, $8.95" and pointed out that wedding dates were available. I turned right, opposite the course, and came immediately to the entrance to the Brookfield Country Club. The tranquil rolling spaces spread out in front of me as I drove in. I felt like a kid again, that kid back at De Haviland. I was listening to Mark Knopfler sing about happily walking through a meadow and stopping under a tree, and I pulled the car over to pay more attention to the music and to watch a foursome of golfers approaching a green. I couldn't identify the emotions coursing through me, but I was sure they had something to do with wanting to travel lightly and easily through life but getting caught up in the commotion. The foursome putted out, and I continued into the parking lot.

Two guys were putting on their golf shoes beside their truck. One golfer wearing jean shorts walked by carrying two cans of beer. Moe came from a course like this, and he landed at the Augusta National Golf Club. He always was a little boy. All he wanted to do was play. His golf clubs were his instruments.

•

I CONSIDER MOE A SUCCESS AT LIVING. He did what he wanted until his health deteriorated to the point where he couldn't do it anymore. "I don't know what my life would have become if I wouldn't have been swinging a golf stick," he told me when he was in his mid-sixties. I'd asked him how he was feeling about things. "I still feel misunderstood," Moe said. "I think I always will, because my story is so different. But I don't let things bother me so much now. I know that I have something that people want, to hit the ball in a repetitious way. What a good feeling, even in countries I've never been they've heard of this guy Moe Norman."

Moe took that feeling to his motel room in Kitchener every night after making his rounds of courses in southern Ontario, courses such as Beaverdale, Brookfield, Century Pines, Rockway. He felt at home at driving ranges, on golf courses and in his car on the open road listening to his tapes.

"It's nice," Moe told me of the motel room where he was living. "I park right against the door. That's what I like. It's beautiful. There's a pop machine right outside, you put a loonie in. No elevator, a nice color TV. I need very little as long as I'm doing what I want to do. I'm the happiest guy on two feet."

Maybe he was.

ACKNOWLEDGMENTS

FIRST, I'D LIKE TO THANK MY EDITOR at ECW Press, Jen Hale, for her understanding of what I was trying to do and for helping me get out of my own way; she knew what I wanted to say even when I wasn't sure how to get there. Thanks also to Jack David at ECW Press for agreeing to meet with me for deli at Pancer's in Toronto, and for his e-mail shortly thereafter asking if I'd like to write this book. I guess pastrami and stories go well together. I appreciate and thank Jen's and Jack's co-workers at ECW who helped in so many ways as we moved toward publication. Then there's Faith Hamlin, my patient and wise agent at Sanford J. Greenburger. She heard the enthusiasm in my voice whenever I spoke about Moe. Thanks, Faith, for spurring me on to write a book I've wanted to write for years.

I am also grateful to the *Globe and Mail* for its support over the years, and its editors' willingness to allow me to write frequently about Moe. Thirty-two years have passed since I suggested a golf column to its then sports editor, Cec Jennings. I wanted to write about all aspects of the game, and Cec invited me to go ahead. His confidence in me meant so much, and set me off on a path I continue to follow. Don Obe, the legendary editor at *Toronto Life* in those days, advised me simply to write what I know when we spoke about a feature article I was working on for the magazine. I doubt that I'd have been able to develop a career as a golf writer had Cec and Don not welcomed the approach I wanted to take.

Colleagues at many publications have indulged my interest in Moe. I wrote about him for publications such as *ScoreGolf, Golf Magazine, Links, Golf Monthly*, and others. Thanks in particular to *ScoreGolf*'s editor Bob Weeks for his friendship and support over the years. My late and great friend and fellow writer Jim Fitchette was a major influence on me. We talked about Moe. We watched Moe. And always, we talked about writing. Along these lines, I thank Harvey Freedenberg, Michael Savoie, Brad Klein, and Norm Mogil for their comments on the manuscript at various stages. I am also indebted to The Ontario Arts Council for its support. The OAC is invaluable to writers. Thanks as well to Golf Canada for granting use of various photos.

I couldn't have gotten here without everything I learned about Moe from his friends and protectors, Gus and Audrey

Maue. I've known this kind couple for years, and each was always there with answers to my questions. Sometimes, as I got closer to finishing this book, I called late at night. I needed to clarify a detail. Gus and Audrey had the answers. Thanks also to Craig Shankland, like Gus a consummate golf professional, for his observations about Moe and for opening his notebook to me. Craig was writing shortly after Moe's death; his notebook was full of insights. Thanks also to Dr. Richard Keefe for taking the time to view a documentary about Moe, and for his keen observations. Thanks as well to Moe's family, and, especially, to his sister Marie and his brother Richard, for the window they provided into their family's life.

Then there's Moe himself. How lucky was I to run into him so many years ago, deep into the last century? How lucky was I that my late father, Percy Rubenstein, who followed and played golf, knew that above all, it's a game that encourages expressions of individuality and idiosyncratic behavior? My dad never laughed at somebody who was different, and Moe sure was different. My dad liked Moe and appreciated the way he hit the golf ball. Moe was okay in his books, which helped me move along a road that has culminated in my writing this book.

My mother, Helen Rubenstein, died in October 2010, just as I was starting this book. I think often of the morning when we sat in the solarium in her condo, and I told her I was going to write a book about my experiences with Moe. Already gravely ill, she smiled, and said, "Really? That's wonderful." I doubt that I would have turned to writing about golf had she, and my father, not encouraged me to go my own way years ago, when the way was not at all clear. I miss them both every day, and I'm grateful to them every minute.

My wife Nell has lived with me for twenty years and with Moe for as many. I spoke with her frequently, even obsessively, about my interest in writing this book. She felt I should. I ran into roadblocks during the writing and often felt discouraged. Nell, a former college English professor, knows good writing, and, with love, she nudged me forward when I wasn't sure I could finish the book. She led me out of the rough and back to the fairway, as she's been doing for twenty years. I'm more than lucky to have Nell in my life. She makes everything possible, even when I think something's impossible.

LORNE RUBENSTEIN has written a golf column for *The Globe and Mail* since 1980. He is a member of the Ontario Golf Hall of Fame and the Canadian Golf Hall of Fame and was given a Sports Media Canada Award for lifetime achievement in 2009. He has won four first-place awards from the Golf Writers Association of America — two for newspaper columns, one for magazine features and one for magazine columns — and one National Magazine Award in Canada.

He is the author of eleven books, including *The Natural Golf Swing* with George Knudson (1988), *A Season in Dornoch: Golf and Life in the Scottish Highlands* (2001) and *Mike Weir: The Road to the Masters* (2003). He lives in Toronto, Ontario, and Jupiter, Florida.